To Geoffrey :—

We love the save cars — and people

Yours

[signature]

More
MOTOR RACING
THE POSTWAR YEARS

More MOTOR RACING
THE POSTWAR YEARS

RIVERS FLETCHER

Foulis

Haynes

A **Foulis** Motoring Book

First published 1991

© A F Rivers Fletcher 1991

Published by:
Haynes Publishing Group
Sparkford, Nr Yeovil
Somerset BA22 7JJ, England

Haynes Publications Inc
861 Lawrence Drive, Newbury Park,
California 91320, USA

A catalogue record for this book
is available from the British Library

ISBN 0 85429 687 5

Library of Congress Catalog Card Number
91–73432

Editor: Robin Read
Design: Robin Read & Associates
Typeset in Times Med Rom 12 pt. and
printed in England by J H Haynes & Co Ltd.

CONTENTS

DEDICATION

Sir Alfred George Beech Owen, CBE, my boss and mentor for twenty momentous years; whose strength, resolve and kindness has benefited not only motor racing, but countless other activities to which this Christian Gentleman gave his time.

FOREWORD

by Sir Peter Masefield
MA; C Eng; Hon. FRAes; FCIT
Chairman, Brooklands Museum Trust

HERE IS a book to be savoured and enjoyed. It is written with insight, humour and an infectious enthusiasm for life in general and for the business of motor sport in particular. I commend it as compulsive reading, and as a sparkling account of a small, but vigorous, contribution to British post–war achievements in industry and venturesome enterprises. With that, it is, also – and almost incidentally – something of a social history of the times and of some of its outstanding personalities.

For more than sixty, crowded years Alec Francis Rivers Fletcher – at the centre of the motoring scene and revelling in a love–affair with motor sport and its people – has enjoyed the affectionate regard of a legion of friends. Now, his story, told with spirit, sets on record a thorough–going account of one man's adventures during the half century from 1939, accompanied and supported by his delightful wife, Penny.

I first met Rivers back in April 1945, when, with Lord Brabazon of Tara, he called at Gwydyr House in Whitehall, then the office of Lord Beaverbrook's "War Cabinet Committee on Post War Air Transport" in Winston Churchill's government. On Lord Beaverbrook's staff, as Secretary of that Committee, I was involved – among much else – with plans for the future of war–time airfields. Brab and Rivers sought help for the post–war restoration of motor–racing in Britain. I am glad that – with "the Beaver's" blessing – I was able to take a positive line on the future of the sport around airfield perimeter tracks – notably at Silverstone. Less easy was support for a new light aircraft engine with which Rivers was ardently involved at that time.

Then, nearly two years later, in January 1947, I met Rivers again at White Waltham Aerodrome where, with the new Minister of Civil Aviation, Lord Nathan, I had been able to arrange a flying display of the latest British and foreign light aircraft, to encourage the design and development of a new generation in this category for Britain. Rivers – with his usual enthusiasm – arrived with the latest British "hopeful" – the Chrislea Ace. It was a brave effort by a small team around a new "Monaco" aero–engine. Sadly, it did not survive the inevitably heavy burden of development costs.

Rivers' remarkable career in subsequent years is delightfully told in this book, against a background of people, places and events which read like a cavalcade of enterprise in the specialist field of light engineering and motor car developments.

Here is, indeed, an inside story recounted with panache and relish against a backdrop of Brooklands, Goodwood, Shelsley Walsh, Prescott and Silverstone; illuminated by a galaxy of people – such as the great "Brab", Bill Boddy, David Brown, Malcolm and Donald Campbell, John Cobb, Ian Connell, Kaye Don, the Dunfee Brothers, George Eyston, Graham Hill, Lord Howe, Raymond Mays, Peter Monkhouse, Sir Alfred Owen, Henry Segrave and Chris Staniland. And, through it, there run like a thread those famous marques of cars – all of them driven with delight by Rivers himself – Alvis, the Bentleys, the BRMs, the Bugattis, the Coopers, the Delages, the ERAs, the Ferraris, the Jaguars, the MGs and a dozen more.

What this enjoyable book reveals yet again is the special fascination which has existed, down the ages, for vehicles of every sort – from the fragile coracles of the Ancient Britons, through the elegant sailing ships of later years, the stately stage–coaches, to steam trains and on, to the age of the motor car and the aeroplane.

With all of that goes, hand–in–hand, the pleasure and the importance – as well as the peculiarities – of the people who have designed, built and operated all those examples of skill, dedication and ingenuity. Life is, indeed, about people – their ambitions, their achievements, their disappointments and their determinations – and, most of all, the enjoyments of their company.

All that is here in full measure – a story of information and happy memories. No less important, it is a faithful reflection of the attitudes and ambitions of the times.

And, of Rivers himself, as Shakespeare said in Richard II:–

> "I count myself in nothing else so happy
> "As..... remembering good friends."

Peter Masefield
Rosehill, Reigate

INTRODUCTION

The Author in his eightieth year.

As this book covers nearly half a century of my life from the age of 27, I have only attempted to recall in any detail the early part when we kept the sport of motor racing alive during the war and got it started again afterwards.

Part I	Chapters 1 to 5. Tells of the bombardment of London and part-time work with the ERA designer, Peter Berthon.
Part II	Chapters 6 to 8. Work with Peter Monkhouse at Monaco's at Watford and the organization of the "Rembrandts" keeping the sport alive during the war.
Part III	Chapters 9 to 11. Motor racing again, the first events in England and Grands Prix on the Continent.
Part IV	Chapters 12 to 16. Our own racing with HRG and MG. New projects for ERA and a National Grand Prix car.

By that time, in 1949, my motor racing activities had already occupied most of twenty years, although five of them were inactive War years. The next forty years, making a Diamond Jubilee of sixty years of motor racing, covers an impossibly long story. Twenty years with BRM from the heartbreaks of the V16 to Graham Hill's World Championship with Grand Prix and vintage racing. Driving nearly every racing model of MG, Bentley, ERA, Bugatti, Jaguar etc. with still no let-up.

How best to cover such ground? My personal history is of no significance, only in respect of its length and breadth. The story of BRM is of real importance and requires a book of its own. Thankfully, the historian, Doug Nye, is telling this in his own book which has the fullest co-operation from all of us involved in the project. I know he will recount this in splendid detail and without bias. I considered it myself but I have been too close and have always been a rather biased sort of chap, an inside raconteur but never an historian. Thus I will only recall some of the highlights and tell some of the stories of the life in which I have been, so far, undeservedly fortunate. A motor racing existence which, despite the inevitable setbacks that are all part of the game, continues to expand after the final chapters of my book:

Part V	Chapters 17 to 22. Joining Alfred Owen and Raymond Mays with BRM. Our Cooper days and a serious HWM-Jaguar accident. Leaving BRM.
Part VI	Chapters 23 to 26. On my own as a consultant. Vintage and historic racing and good future prospects.

ACKNOWLEDGEMENTS

My first and greatest thanks are to my wife, Penny, who has had to cope with yet another book – papers all over the house, her domestic life blighted by far too much husbandly toil and travel at a time, in my 80th year when I should have been properly retired ages ago.

My thanks go to numerous friends who have remembered details and dates etc. As previously, I have relied on the good memories of John and Isobel Willis, Ronnie Mountford and the editors of motor magazines. For this book, my special thanks go to Sir Peter Masefield, first of all for his invaluable help with regard to the details in the Battle of Britain, and for doing me the great honour of consenting to write the Foreword. This is so apt because it was he who made it possible for us to use war–time airfields for motor–racing so soon after the end of the war; and now he masterminds the restoration of much of the old Brooklands track for a live museum for the motor, motorcycle and aircraft industries.

I have to thank the many friends who have given me photographs used in the book: George Monkhouse, Louis Klemantaski, Guy Griffiths, Charles Dunn, Clive Taylor, Terrence Brettell, Alan Cox, Charles Rangeley-Wilson, Bruce Bamford and many others who cannot be identified because those pictures have been mounted or pasted into albums preventing their identification.

Enthusiastic help from Shirley Monro-Dickson and the rest of our team has enabled me to complete the story up to the beginning of 1991. But the saga continues. My final thanks go to the book's Editor, my friend Robin Read.

PART I

WARTIME ENTHUSIASM

The bombardment of London and part- time work with the ERA designer, Peter Berthon

CHAPTER ONE

My first volume of autobiography *Mostly Motor Racing*, told my story to the outbreak of the Second World War in September 1939. At that time, I was with a small company called Shelsley Motors Limited, with Raymond Mays, Peter Berthon and Lance Prideaux-Brune. We were producing the Raymond Mays Special car at the old ERA works at Mays' home, Eastgate House in Bourne, Lincolnshire; our London headquarters were at Prideaux-Brune's Winter Garden Garages. We were racing Mays' ERA No. R4D and were coming to the end of a very successful season, but with war clouds overshadowing everything. I was about to be engaged to be married to my girlfriend, Penny.

In the last chapter of *Mostly Motor Racing* I wrote, "It was generally believed that if war was declared there would be an immediate air raid on London. To that end, there was a drive to build up an auxiliary fire service in the Greater London area ... thinking it would be great fun to drive a fire engine, I enlisted ..." This is the way I finished the book:

Penny and I were driving back from Mattins at Finchley, on the Great North Road towards Barnet, when we heard for the first time the dreaded wailing of the air raid warning. Police and wardens directed us off the main road to an air raid shelter near by. Though there was no raid on that morning, as it was a false alarm, nevertheless it was for real. We were at war and our world of motor racing and much else was at a halt. What of the dream? So far so good, I had had a lot of luck and I was only 27 – was there a future? Could there be motor racing again, and would I be there? I wondered and hoped with the optimism of comparative youth, and believed that somehow or other the rest of the dream would come true.

The start of the war was not at all as expected and there was no instant air raid on London. However, all Fire Service personnel were instructed to report to their stations forthwith. As I was listed as a driver for the London area, I was put on permanent full alert. Contact with the Manpower Board and reference to interviews that Peter Berthon and I had had, confirmed that we should remain where we were: I as a fireman and Peter working on Ministry of Aircraft Production contracts he had already started at Bourne. We were told that we would

*The East Barnet Fire
Brigade regulars.*

be notified if and when we were required as technical officers for the armed services.

For me, life was drills, lectures and building up and equipping fire service substations in our area of North London. A great number of men in the Auxiliary Fire Service came from the building and construction industry, so we were well placed for that work.

For quite a long time I saw no one except my Fire Service colleagues. There was no contact with our world of motor racing. The *Autocar, Motor, Light Car and Cycle Car* and *Motor Sport* gave what news there was of personalities in thin, rather brief publications. All the principal motor clubs closed down for the duration of the war.

This book is mainly about my involvement with motor racing, so I will not attempt to write much about the war itself. My war was completely inglorious and relatively safe compared with that of most of my motor racing friends. I will not attempt to recount the countless acts of bravery and the tragic deaths suffered by sailors, soldiers and airmen from the world of motor racing. So many of the great drivers of the 1920s and 1930s were killed, as were countless young men who formed the happy band of enthusiasts, described as "the right crowd and no crowding", at Brooklands events.

I will only try to tell how some of us, still based in Britain, gradually got together and kept something going throughout the war years. First and foremost was our technical press. These journals were all splendid and demonstrated that they cared so much "beyond the call of duty", and certainly beyond the commercialism of their trade.

Sammy Davis, "Casque" of *Autocar*, was I think the best motor racing journalist of his day. He was of course one of our greatest sports car drivers, too, a winner with Bentley at Le

Mans and in many other cars at Brooklands and elsewhere. Sammy's attitude to the war must have been almost unique: he really did rather like it! That sounds nonsense today, but I knew Sammy very well indeed and I am convinced that, on balance, he liked and enjoyed war more that he hated it. Of course he deplored the tragedies and misery and was, at heart, the kindest man; but something in Sammy could not help enjoying a war.

As a young man, he had fought and been wounded in the First World War and lost many friends; but he revelled in the excitement and the chance to do or die for his country. His personal stories of that war were just as enthralling as his accounts of Le Mans, but were never documented. It was not surprising that Sammy used every wangle and trick to get back into the Army again in 1939. He managed it, of course, despite his age.

A keen youngster took Sammy's place at the sports desk of *Autocar* for a time. However, the much senior H S Lindfield, who I knew well was in charge of road tests and kept the sport alive with a regular column called "Talking of Sports Cars". Enthusiastic readers contributed stories about their cars and Lindfield added his own comments from his vast road test experience. The series carried on right through the war and beyond. Later journalists, and lastly Ted Eves, continued with the series until quite recently. If it were ever possible to collate all those "Talking of Sports Cars" pieces into a book, it would make a very interesting publication.

Rodney de Burgh Walkerly, "Grande Vitesse" of *Motor*, joined the Army soon after the outbreak of war, but Laurence Pomeroy Junior, then technical editor, and "Bunny" Tubbs jointly took over the sporting side of *Motor* with great effect.

In *Light Car and Cycle Car*, Denis May had been looking after the sporting side as "The Blower". He was soon in the Army so the editor himself, Eric Findon, kept in touch with the sport.

However, the man whose war efforts on our behalf were absolutely staggering was William Boddy, the editor – and almost everything else too – of *Motor Sport*. Almost single-handed, Bill Boddy kept this magazine going and improved it throughout the war years, despite every difficulty. Bill is unique, a "one-off". His love for our sport is his life, for which we are all thankful.

For a long time the Fire Service in the London area had little to do. A lot of drill and exercises taught us to cope with the wonderful little Coventry-Climax pumps and we became adept at rushing up and down ladders and handling the powerful bucking and whipping hoses that projected jets of water further than seemed possible.

From our motor racing world, there was Denis Evans in charge of the AFS in his area of Wandsworth in South London; Desmond Scannell was a mobilizing officer, as was Philip Mayne (ERA team manager), who was in charge of an area surrounded by RAF airfields and likely to have to cope with a lot of raids. Jack Fry, who with David Fry and Dick Caesar, had developed the Freikaiserwagen ("Fry-Caesar-car", an Anglo-German pun), was the envy of us all, driving his 3/4½ Bentley (an H M Bentley rebuild) with his crew and towing the Coventry-Climax pump with great verve.

The war drifted on rather quietly in Britain and not very well on the Continent. Initial hope for a quick and decisive victory for the Allies soon evaporated. We almost lived with our gas masks; the nightly blackout was rigidly enforced, as was severe rationing of nearly everything including, of course, petrol.

Driving at night in the blackout with only 2 inch-diameter sidelights shining through a 2 inch thickness of newspaper and a tiny pencil beam from a headlamp mask, severely curtailed your speed. From a motoring point of view, a bright moonlit night was a godsend. I had an amusing letter from Lord Howe, an RNVR Commodore and also president of the British Racing Drivers' Club and the ERA Club. He had one of his two Fiat 500 Topolinos with him in Glasgow. He wrote saying that he was marrying again and that he was driving his young bride-to-be in the Fiat in the blackout flat out; this was the nearest thing to showing her racing on the track. Having travelled with "the Old Man" in his racing cars on the road in daylight, my heart went out to that girl! Apparently she loved it, so Lord Howe was admirably suited.

ERA was completely closed down and all the staff were swallowed up into war work; the technicians of course were eagerly grabbed by the leading engineering companies. Raymond Mays' wool business in Bourne, which we had regarded as very much secondary to ERA, was now very much his full-time occupation. Peter Berthon was sent to Tony Lago, at the French Talbot works in Suresnes, on an aircraft project.

A meagre basic petrol ration enabled drivers to do only a little private motoring, so many men with thirsty sports cars bought

The fifth Earl Howe (known in pre-war motor racing circles as "the Old Man"), RNVR Commodore HMS Osprey at Glasgow, with one of his Fiat Topolinos.

Fiat 500s or Austin Sevens for most of their journeys and reserved their interesting cars for something special. The trouble was that for most of us there was nothing special, absolutely no events at all. I saw Forrest Lycett driving a Fiat 500 instead of his 8-litre Bentley and Peter Clark was using a gas-producer plant to run an old Delage. Most racing cars were laid up and many were taken to locations in the depths of the country away from likely bomb damage in the cities. We reckoned that Raymond Mays' ERA R4D was just about as safe at Bourne as anywhere and all his Specials were stored away from London. Captain John (later Sir John) Black, who had been using one, stored it at his home near Leamington Spa.

Prince Chula and his cousin "B. Bira", being members of the royal house of neutral Siam, were not allowed to have any part in the war. Their cars, two ERAs and a Maserati, were transferred to safekeeping at Rock in Cornwall, where they were established for the duration.

Barrett, from the ERA drawing office and Percy Pugh, Humphrey Cook's personal mechanic, were in Bristol on aircraft production. A committee member of the ERA Club, Nick Pringle, wrote to me from Cambridge saying that he wished he was at home in the Irish Republic, which was a neutral country, where there was plenty of motoring and club activity. There was even a possibility of some racing and certainly a speed hillclimb where McCarthy made fastest time of the day in his MG K3. Motor racing continued in America and Italy. There was a press report of a sort of shortened Mille Miglia in Italy, in which all our old friends in Alfa Romeos and Maseratis were running. Somehow it seemed quite unreal and unbelievable to us: it was so far away from the world in which we now lived – it did not seem right.

Everyone, male and female, was engaged in some sort of war work. My girlfriend Penny became secretary to the local Food Ministry office. Gradually, very gradually, I made contact with some of my motor racing friends and learned of their whereabouts and activities. As all the principal motor clubs had closed down for the duration of the war, there was a dreadful void in that there was practically no contact among us. One club, the 750 MC, carried on under its secretary S H Capon, so there were a few meetings in this category, but sparsely attended because the club was a national one and its members spread all over the country.

Before the war, with Raymond Mays and Lord Howe at the ERA works at Bourne, I had met J T C Moore-Brabazon, the pioneer racing driver and flying man. Always known as "Brab", he was a legendary character, a leading light in the administration of the Brooklands Automobile Racing Club and the RAC motoring organization. He was best known as an ace tobogganist on the Cresta run. "Brab", who was the first pilot to have a Royal Aero Club flying certificate in 1910, was highly placed in the Air Ministry.

Another friend of mine, Charles Matkin, bought a new Vauxhall Fourteen. His position in the London County Council enabled him to pick a special number plate, so his Vauxhall was registered FLY 1, which he chose as a nice, easily remembered identification. When I told "Brab" about this, he said he would just love to have FLY 1 himself. Charles Matkin was quite agreeable, so a deal was done. "Brab" bought the Vauxhall and later transferred the plate to his streamlined Fiat. So, long before the era of personalized number plates, Lt Col Moore-Brabazon was seen at the wheel of the most appropriate FLY 1.

From time to time when on leave in London I did meet a few kindred souls, had lunch with Anthony Heal and Sam Clutton, visited the *Autocar* to see H S Lindfield, and the Temple Press to meet Laurence Pomeroy Junior and Eric Findon. Nevertheless, we all felt very lost and alone without the great majority of our friends.

Air raids in our area were very sporadic, but grim enough when they came and proved the worth of our fire-fighting equipment and experience. Once when I was walking with Penny in the middle of the day during an air raid alert a lone German

Above left:
Lord Brabazon's streamlined Fiat to which he transferred the FLY 1 plate.

Above right:
Lieutenant-Colonel J T C Moore-Brabazon and his wife, dogs and the Vauxhall FLY 1.

bomber dropped a stick of anti-personnel bombs right in our path. Hearing them coming down, we dropped to the ground, lying face down while one bomb fell 20 yards to the rear of us and the next only 10 yards in front of us on the footpath, making big holes and scattering a lot of earth, but not hurting us at all. That was our nearest squeak so far.

All the fire alarms in our area operated direct to our watchroom in the Fire Station, the nerve centre of our operation. Percy Collings, one of my new friends in the Auxiliary Fire Service, and I were appointed mobilizing officers. We were therefore based in the watchroom, so we only joined crews for the larger fires. Throughout the country the AFS was getting organized to cope with the massive air attacks that were expected at any time.

There were two sorts of firebombs used by the Luftwaffe. The first type was the thermite incendiary, only 18 inches long and quite thin; its pointed head penetrated roofs and burst inside. Many thousands of these thermite bombs could be carried in each bomber. The second type was the oilbomb, much bigger and heavier. This did not penetrate so well but sprayed out burning oil when it exploded. Its skin was of a magnesium alloy like the Elektron castings we used at the Bentley works. I remembered from my apprentice days there how the filings from Elektron castings used to flare up if they were ignited as they fell through the air. Now the same thing was happening again when the oilbombs exploded – a poignant memory.

Besides the main appliance, which was a two- or three-year old Leyland, we had at our AFS headquarters a small fleet of private cars for towing the pumps. The gems in our fleet were three vintage sports cars: a Diatto, a Th. Schneider and a 3-litre Delage, all supplied by a vintage enthusiast in the RAF, John Maw.

I admit that I pulled rank and mostly used the Delage myself. The winter of 1939-40 was a very severe one with a lot of snow and ice. I soon found out that trying to skid round corners with the Delage and a pump on tow was not on: I bent a towbar and buckled a wheel on a pump and could not think of any good excuse for my mishap. Although I drove the Delage for most Fire Service duties, I had to use my own Riley Nine tourer for personal transport. Penny and I enjoyed a very limited amount of winter motoring.

Raymond Mays forsook his Bentley and did all his essential motoring in a very nice Rover Fourteen sports saloon and his mother took to another Rover, a two-door Ten. Both cars were in black with pale-blue upholstery, like Ray's Bentley and his ERA.

Above right:
Penny with the Riley, snow and wartime livery.

Above left:
AFS "B" Watch, with the Th. Schneider.

Left:
At the wheel of the Delage.

CHAPTER TWO

During the early part of the Second World War there were some very sad deaths in the world of motor racing, some from natural causes and others, of course, in action: E V Ebblewhite ("Ebby"), the famous Brooklands handicapper; S F Edge, perhaps the most famous pioneer racing driver at Brooklands; Colonel Lindsay Lloyd, Clerk of the Course at Brooklands; Colonel R E Crompton, RAC Competition Committee member and a director of Crompton Parkinson, the electrical engineers – he was close to my family, as my grandfather and an uncle had been co-directors with him. Others lost in this period were Teddy Rayson, who raced an 1100 cc Maserati; T E Rose-Richards, one of the finest drivers, a regular team driver with Talbot and Lagonda and co-driver with John Cobb, winning the 500 at Brooklands in the Napier-Railton. Luis Fontes was another star driver, a surprise winner of the 1933 International Trophy at Brooklands, and subsequently a very successful team driver with Lagonda. His racing career ended tragically with a dreadful road accident and he was killed while flying in the RAF.

I started to get letters and telephone calls from drivers and enthusiasts complaining that they had no means of meeting. Servicemen on leave rang me and the press as well, pleading that something should be arranged so that, at least, they could get together from time to time. I called my friends in the offices of *Autocar* and *Motor*. Lindfield told me the same story and Laurence Pomeroy, always known as "Pom", and "Bunny" Tubbs said that they felt that something should be done, but no one came forward with a concrete suggestion.

When I was on night duty with the AFS, Anthony Heal and Sam Clutton, leading members of the Vintage Sports Car Club and John Wyer, the London manager of Solex Carburettors, came to be my regular lunch companions at Viani's Restaurant in Charlotte Street, just off Tottenham Court Road. They all told the same story – with the principal clubs closed down, there was no method by which enthusiasts could contact one another. So I suggested to "Pom" of *Motor* and Lindfield of *Autocar* that they should put notices in their journals saying that Rivers Fletcher would be at a certain place in London at a fixed time on a fixed future date, in the hope that any other enthusiasts might join me for a drink. My thoughts were that a few fellow members of the ERA Club, of which I was the chairman, would see the notice and join me; and since I knew so many drivers, officials and enthusiasts in the other motor clubs, some might come along so that we could start something more concrete.

After further meetings with Clutton, Heal, "Pom", and "Bunny" Tubbs, I wrote to the motoring press fixing a definite date and place: the first Saturday in each month at St Stephen's Tavern at Westminster. We had used St Stephen's Tavern for some early ERA Club meetings and it was conveniently placed and easily located on the Embankment, close to Westminster Bridge. H S Lindfield of *Autocar*, "Pom" and "Bunny" Tubbs of *Motor*, Bill Boddy of *Motor Sport*, and Eric Findon of *Light Car and Cycle Car* all gave wonderful support with plenty of publicity. I had completely committed myself, so I kept my fingers crossed.

On the first Saturday of July 1940 we started the first wartime enthusiasts' gathering. It was a great success, better than I dared hope: about 40 people turned up, half of them in uniform. They started to come in from about 6.30 pm. Some had made long journeys from other parts of the country, obtaining special leave from their units. We heard how so many other enthusiasts yearned for some sort of contact, new friendships were made and old ones cemented. Some of us played the race game as built at Brooklands by Desmond Tilley and Tappenden, using little scale models and a roulette wheel. Naturally, however, the evening was mostly spent talking with kindred spirits and hearing news of other drivers and enthusiasts. All present said they would attend the next meeting in a month's time and most promised they would be bringing other enthusiasts as well – so we had started something worthwhile.

The press reported the meeting as "the ERA Club Gathering", even though the club had officially closed down. The second meeting was even better, with a larger attendance. Among the newcomers were Stuart Wilton, the MG driver and Philip Turner, now in RAF uniform. Sam Green, the secretary of the ERA Club, was absent because he was on duty with the Royal Army Ordnance Corps. Peter Clark, whose HRG sports car had been so successful at Le Mans, was present and carried a message from his co-driver, Marcus Chambers, who was in the Royal Navy. I had news that Peter Berthon had returned from Paris and was working again in England.

My job in the AFS was not all that demanding, consisting mainly of waiting for something to happen. Most of our drills and exercises took place during our day shifts. As we have seen, being on the night shift meant that I could meet some of my motoring friends in London. Peter Berthon had now moved to London and had a drawing office in Piccadilly, where he worked day and night on several projects for the Ministry of Aircraft Production and the Admiralty. He was desperate for more draughtsmen; two he wanted had gone off to Rotol at Bristol and, like everyone else on such projects, he was overloaded with work. He asked if I could work for him during the daytime when I was on a night shift. Of course, it would be quite unofficial:

the regulations required me to work full-time in the Fire Service. Peter was in partnership with Richard Booth (I had got to know him at Brooklands along with the Talbot driver Bill Esplen). Their company, Heath, Booth & Co, would pay me something out of petty cash. It seemed to me that it was a good idea and so began a very hectic period. With one other draughtsman we coped in a very small drawing office on the third floor above a toy shop in the Burlington Arcade. Heath, Booth & Co took contracts to supply components and small assemblies, mostly required for the RAF and the Fleet Air Arm. They had a subsidiary company, Mortimer Engineering, at Islington. Peter Berthon, using a Fiat 500, divided his time between the two companies.

We had a large number of subcontractors working for us, mostly small companies not used to the sort of work now required. They were furniture makers, toy makers, ironmongers, building contractors, makers of musical instruments and some garages. All were keen to be engaged on war work, but most of them did not know how to get started. We had to assess their abilities, their plant and personnel and often had to add to or modify their plant. We had to design and make jigs and tools and inspect their products, as well as supply and deliver the material and finished products.

The size of the job was staggering, but this sort of thing was going on all over the country. It produced some great men and, inevitably, some terrible misfits. Stupendous results were achieved and a few awful mistakes made. Peter Berthon and I were lucky in that we worked with Richard Booth, someone with tremendous drive and enthusiasm, who was ruthless in his zest for results. Unorthodox in his methods, he took some dreadful risks but got away with them.

My first jobs were designing gauges so that our subcontractors could check their products. Of course, everything had to be to AID or Admiralty specifications. Since most of the staff were quite new to this work, it all had to be as simple as possible and foolproof as well. I used my Riley Nine to drive around to the various works and Richard Booth provided the necessary petrol coupons. Since my work was quite unofficial, he could not get the petrol through the correct channels and I dare not think where he really acquired the coupons!

For my drawing office work, I used techniques I had learned from Mr Sewell when I was an apprentice at Bentley Motors Limited and later at ERAs working for Peter Berthon. In both of these companies I had been criticized for my slapdash, hastily executed drawings and untidy lettering. Now nobody worried about such things and the fact that I was a speedy worker was very advantageous. Berthon still raised an eyebrow from time to time at the untidiness of my work, but he complimented me on the quick and accurate results achieved.

The war news got worse and worse. Jokes like "hanging the washing on the Siegfried Line" became a little sick. More and more of our aircraft were shot down and the news from the front on the Continent became tragic, culminating in the evacuation of British and French forces from Dunkirk.

The whole nation responded to Winston Churchill's grim but

splendid words to be ready to fight the foe to the last ditch. There was tremendous activity in all forms of defence, including our Auxiliary Fire Service, but no sign of actual invasion of our shores.

My daytime work with Heath, Booth & Co seemed so much more important than the nightly standing by and exercises in the Fire Service. I did a lot more designing of jigs and tools to suit the varied plant in our companies, finding that the young women operators were every bit as quick to adjust to the new jobs as the men.

In the summer of 1940 we had been at war for nearly a year: we were used to it. For most of my friends and relations, except those in the armed services, there was a pattern of living not too different from peacetime. People got on with their daily lives. Mothers pushed babies in prams, boys played cricket and football, folk fell in and out of love, marriages were made and broken, but all to a backcloth of wartime uncertainty.

It was the uncertainty that made all the difference. In a sense we lived from day to day. That sounds rather dramatic, but remember that at that time we did not really know how and

when we could win the war. We only knew that we would not give in – and that is not quite the same thing. Although there was some bombing of ports, attacks on London were as yet sporadic, often by single aircraft. Sometimes I saw dogfights, with Spitfires and Hurricanes attacking German bombers, but none of the planes came down in our area. Quite a lot of the people who had fled from London on the outbreak of war were coming back. A poison gas attack was still a possibility, at least, and most people carried their gas masks everywhere.

Wartime shot of Penny dispensing refreshment after a bombing raid.

CHAPTER THREE

I have said that I would not attempt to write in any great detail about the course of the war. However, to convey something of the part of it that I was actively involved in, I will briefly outline the story of the Battle of Britain. I am not a flying man so what follows is not written out of any first-hand experience of the war in the air, but was researched through talks with RAF men and draws its information from several reputable authorities.

After Dunkirk and the fall of France in June 1940, the Luftwaffe occupied airfields all along the French and Belgian coasts and in the Netherlands.

Britain seemed to be out of the war, with little to stop Hitler walking in and setting up a pro-Nazi puppet government. He did not wish to destroy Britain at this stage – but he misjudged the stubborn British mentality and waited in vain for any sign of surrender.

A seaborne invasion (code-named Sealion) was therefore decided upon, but the Germans had first to obtain air supremacy over southern England to be assured of success. By late July 1940 they could bring to bear 656 serviceable aircraft on targets in this region; the Royal Air Force had 493 fighters available. The first part of Sealion envisaged concentrated attacks on fighter airfields, ports and convoys, as well as on aircraft factories in the south of England. The accomplishment of these aims would also demonstrate the futility of Great Britain continuing the war.

The main combat aircraft used on the German side in the Battle of Britain were the twin-engined Heinkel He 111, Dornier Do 17 and Junkers Ju 88 bombers, and the single-engined Ju 87 Stuka dive bomber; their fighters were the single-engined Messerschmitt Bf 109 and the twin-engined Bf 110. The best of these machines were powered by Daimler-Benz engines: shades of the pre-war Mercedes racing cars.

Britain had Sydney Camm's great Hawker Hurricane and Reginald Mitchell's famous Supermarine Spitfire. Hurricanes were assembled at Brooklands and flown to their squadrons after flight-testing by a small Hawker team led by Major George Bulman.

Affection for and loyalty to aircraft types were similar to those bestowed on sports cars and often came from the same people. Friends of mine in the Air Transport Auxiliary who made delivery flights of both Hurricanes and Spitfires preferred the latter; most RAF fighter pilots fiercely supported their own aircraft, Hurricane or Spitfire.

Luftwaffe attacks on airfields caused many casualties among Royal Air Force and Women's Auxiliary Air Force personnel. Manston, right on the coast, had a particularly bad time. At one point damage to fighter bases was so severe that in southern England only two, Tangmere and Kenley, were in operation. German bombing of aircraft factories varied in its effectiveness.

After suffering considerable losses, the German command took the momentous decision at the beginning of September to switch the attack to London, in the expectation that the whole of Britain's fighter strength would be drawn into its defence. Bombing the capital would, it was hoped, bring a speedy end to British resistance: Hitler had the examples of Warsaw and Rotterdam to encourage him.

The first massed attack, on 7 September, left London's East End and Dockland in flames. Subsequently, although the Blitz on London went on for night after night for months, it failed to undermine morale or induce surrender.

Victory in the crucial Battle of Britain came to RAF Fighter Command because of the skills and devotion of the people who designed and built the aircraft, of its ground staff, both men and women, and of the civilian services – but, above all, because of the enduring courage of its pilots. Daily, hourly they faced terrible injury, disfigurement and death. Often they did so in the light-hearted manner of sportsmen, of competitors in motor racing and every exciting or dangerous activity. Cheerful RAF slang hid or camouflaged the fear no one cared to show.

It was strange to reflect that among the enemy pilots there might well be the Mercedes and Auto Union men we had liked and admired so recently at Donington, Monte Carlo, the Nürburgring, the Avus, Monza and other circuits.

The Battle of Britain was just one phase of the Second World War, involving a relatively small segment of the combating forces for quite a short period – but it was of great eventual importance.

As it happened, Penny and I were in the front line as all this started. I was able to see quite a lot of it and even play an exciting, albeit insignificant part in the Auxiliary Fire Service (AFS) in the second phase of the Battle of Britain: the Blitz on London. As we have seen, there were three weeks of continuous air attacks on RAF airfields, but the London Fire Service was scarcely involved. On 7 September, I was on 48 hours' leave from the AFS. Penny and I drove to London in the Riley to see a revue called "Up and Doing" at the Saville Theatre. The cast included Leslie Henson, to whom I had once sold a car, Binnie Hale, Cyril Richard, Stanley Holloway and Marie Burke's very attractive daughter, Patricia. The orchestra was under the direction of Carroll Gibbons.

During the show an air raid warning sounded but, as this was very usual and most often would be quickly followed by the all

Programme of "Up and Doing" revue.

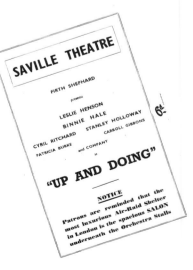

clear, nobody took any notice. On the programme there was a notice: "Patrons are reminded that the most luxurious air raid shelter in London is the spacious salon underneath the orchestra stalls". This time, however, we started to hear gunfire and falling bombs – quite a lot of them and fairly near. Still, very few people moved out of their seats. During the last act the bombing became much heavier and you could scarcely hear the words and music above the din.

At the conclusion of the performance, an announcement was made from the stage saying that a very heavy air raid was in progress. People could remain in the theatre if they wished. Carroll Gibbons went to the microphone and announced that he and some of the orchestra would continue to play for our entertainment. Some people left the theatre and quite a lot went down to the shelter. As I already knew Carroll Gibbons, I walked to the front of the stalls and had a chat with him and the orchestra played a couple of tunes that I requested. It was all very informal, casual and, I thought, rather delightful.

The bombing and gunfire continued, no better and no worse; so, after a time, Penny and I decided that we would go outside and see what it was like. It was very noisy and a lot of the noise seemed rather close. The whole of the sky was red and we could see flames reaching upwards in the east. We walked towards St Martins Lane, where we had left our car in a garage. However, we were turned back by police and air raid wardens, who told us that the entrance to St Martins Lane was blocked with falling masonry. Then a bomb came down only a street or two away from us and we hurried back to the comparative shelter of the theatre foyer.

Fire over London.

It looked as though the whole of the city was on fire. Although I was on leave, I reckoned that I should report for duty as early as possible the next morning; but it was impossible to do so that night. The only thing we could do would be to stay the night in London at a hotel (a heaven-sent excuse!).

Our best bet was the Regent Palace Hotel, so close at hand; but there I was told that it was full. However, there was still some accommodation left at the Strand Palace, a similar establishment in the same group. I managed to get a taxi and the driver said he thought the road from Piccadilly to the Strand was clear. He said he would take us as far as the Strand Palace, but no further east, as he reckoned that everything was on fire beyond St Paul's Cathedral. On the way we had to make a diversion, as an office building was partly demolished, blocking the road at Lower Regent Street. At the Strand Palace, I very daringly requested a room for "Mr and Mrs Smith" and got one on the top floor. With some difficulty we telephoned our respective parents out at Barnet, explaining the situation, which they fully appreciated because they could see the vivid red sky over London and could hear the continuous gunfire and bombing. What could they say? We assured them that we would find good shelter in some basement overnight.

In fact that is what happened because, on reaching our bedroom on the top floor, a nearby bomb shook the place so violently that we decided to collect pillows and some bedclothes and depart immediately to the lower ground floor restaurant, hoping that we could bed down there. It was very crowded and noisy, with no room at any table and lots of people standing around and sitting in corners. I spotted an alcove underneath some stairs, so we tucked our bedclothes and pillows into that space and snuggled down together wrapped in an eiderdown. Down there, in the basement, you could not hear so much of the gunfire and bombing and we soon fell asleep. Penny tells me that she awoke in the early hours of the morning to hear a man saying, "Look at those bloody kids under the stairs!"

That was the first night of the London Blitz. As soon as morning came, I hastened back to the Fire Service. Everyone was on duty from then on, night and day. The continuous bombing of London by night has been extensively documented, and also the role of the Fire Service. There is little I can add to that story. Most of us worked in small units of six or seven men and sometimes we operated with quite large groupings of units under a mobilizing officer. From the second night on, there were so many buildings on fire that when we drove into the City of London we merely picked a building that seemed likely to be worth saving; if possible one in which there might be people to be rescued.

Whereas on exercises in the less urgent past there had been some friction between police, firemen and air raid wardens, there was now complete co-operation between the various services. During the worst of the bombing and the fiercest fires, there was an almost happy and cheerful atmosphere. It seems that there is a need for mankind, or at least the British, to find humour and a forced cheerfulness to hide the grimness of the worst situations.

All this was something quite new. Crews were sent from East Barnet to report at stations and substations at Barking, Hackney, Wanstead and Forest Gate. Some were out for 24 or 36 hours. Few had any sleep, because the London Docks were the focal point of the Blitz and there was continuous bombing and gunfire. There was no question of any blackout because everything was lit up by the enormous fires. Huge office blocks and factories close to the docks were completely gutted and yet still blazing away. Searchlights probed the sky, often catching and holding bombers being attacked by our fighters. One aircraft, engulfed in flames, crashed about two blocks away: I believe it was one of ours. A double-decker bus was standing almost on its tail, up against the wall of an office block. There was water everywhere, and miles and miles of hosepipe, some of it burst by bombs, shrapnel or traffic.

I saw a young station officer standing on top of a telephone booth giving instructions through a loudhailer. He must have been there for hours, with his face black and absolutely soaking wet. Yet, somehow or other, there was some order. Instructions were given and obeyed; more water was pumped into that building and pumps were switched to another factory; firemen went up and down turntable ladders, which were switched as directed.

One of our leading firemen ("leading fireman" was a rank in the Fire Service) was injured by a large piece of shrapnel that missed his helmet but embedded itself in his shoulder. If a bomb landed anywhere near you no sort of protection could be any help, but the steel helmets certainly protected your head from shrapnel, which could be quite substantial.

A large piece of shrapnel was embedded in the scuttle of the Riley, just in front of the windscreen; so I left it there as a sort of trophy.

Items of drill, words of command that we had learned parrot fashion, came to life in the tumult of the Blitz. I found that we did not feel tired or really frightened – but sometimes quite hungry or thirsty as mobile canteens appeared from nowhere with cheerful members of the Women's Voluntary Service dispensing tea and food.

The regular peacetime firemen showed complete mastery. They were absolutely professional, demonstrating skills that years of training and experience had taught them. We comparative newcomers of the AFS struggled to keep up with them. Some of us were nearly as quick up the ladders and in directing the hoses as the regulars, but most of us stumbled about in our heavy boots with our equipment and found it rather hard going.

Some fantastic rescues were achieved. Two men who had been on fire-watching duty on top of a warehouse were completely cut off as the wharf was engulfed in flames. A regular fireman on the highest turntable ladder brought them down safely, one after the other, choking through the smoke and with flames licking their clothes.

Fire over London: another view.

Day after day, night after night the Blitz carried on. Every day German planes dropped incendiaries to stoke up the fires to guide the bombers on their night raids. Great numbers of women and children living in East London took trams and buses to destinations further out in the suburbs, returning each morning to their homes, hoping to find them intact.

After about a month, the attack moved more to the West End and on some nights to other parts of London, so we were constantly regrouping our resources. There was seldom enough water at hand.

The greatest damage caused in air raids in our own area came from landmines. Some fell in open country doing little harm, but on three occasions houses were hit and completely demolished, with properties on each side severely damaged. Only a few people were killed outright, but many more were injured. Our Fire Service was called out each time. The main appliance and the back-up team of AFS personnel with auxiliary pumps attended. However, they were not as much needed as were the ambulance and first-aid teams.

Badly bombed homes, often with an outside wall demolished, looked like doll's houses with furniture and pictures still in position. This reminded me of the only war damage that I remembered seeing during the First World War. I must have been about five years old when a house was bombed in Totteridge Lane about two miles from our home and two or three people were killed. That had looked like a broken doll's house and had an eerie fascination for me. I had to look at it, even though I was frightened by what had happened.

There were some very distressing sights after landmines had been dropped: bodies, severed limbs and a lot of blood. Assessing reactions to such things was very difficult. Sometimes the

toughest and most worldly types could not cope at all, while
some of the gentlest and sweetest people turned out to be at their
very best under those conditions. It was lucky that Penny and
her mother, having to be on hand at air raids and their
aftermath in our location, were able to cope very well, taking it
all in their stride.

The Auxiliary Fire Service allowed you minimum periods of
leave to recoup your strength. Of course, during the Blitz no
private visits to London for war work were possible for me
because my priority at that time had to be the Fire Service. That
was the pattern of life until the 8 December; then, just as
suddenly as it started, the London Blitz ended. There was no
more nightly bombing and only stray daytime bombers. Within a
week, Richard Booth was on the phone. "What's the matter,
Rivers? Are you sick or something? The bombing is over; stop
playing fireman and get back to some real work." I reported to
my station officer and he, rather reluctantly, put me back to
normal hours. This enabled me to do two weeks' work for
Heath, Booth & Co, followed by one week for the Fire Service
and I continued in this way for some time.

London had been in the front line of the war, with hundreds
of people killed every night. Yet, in a very strange way, it was a
happy time. We thought things could only get better and nearly
everyone seemed determined to be more cheerful and more
anxious to display British grit than anyone else. Shops blasted
and almost written off displayed humorous notices apologizing to
their customers.

With so much bomb damage to some of our subcontractors,
new suppliers had to be found to maintain and increase our
production. I worked closely with Peter Berthon on the design of
new jigs and tools. I came to have a great regard for his genius,
his quick and often brilliant ideas. At the same time, I came to
understand and tolerate his dreadful timekeeping and impossible
hours. He was never punctual for a meeting, however important;
on the other hand, he would work night and day to finish a job.
This was most unfair on staff who had started their jobs at the
proper time.

It all reminded me of ERA at Bourne, where Raymond Mays
got the best and the most out of Peter because of their excellent
rapport. At Heath, Booth & Co, Richard also certainly knew
how to handle Peter and we formed rather a good team.

Several months of this hectic life, with my poor old Riley
living outside all the time and making high-speed runs to and
from London and our subcontractors in the suburbs, completely
wore it out. It soon started to drink oil at a prodigious rate and
the fabric body came to pieces. Regretfully, I sold it for not
much more than a song and bought a remarkably well-preserved
1927 Austin Seven two-seater. With no personal car of my own
to tow a pump, I had a valid reason to use the Vanden Plas
Delage for Fire Service duties. The Austin Seven was eminently
suitable for my journeys for the firm – and, of course, was very
economical. Peter Berthon soon tired of his Fiat 500 and changed
to a Lancia Aprilia, which we both enjoyed very much: fantastic
cornering and four top gears! So you lived in the gear-box.

*Penny outside Rothiemay
House with the 1927 Austin
Seven two-seater.*

CHAPTER FOUR

During the London Blitz, my first-Saturday-of-the-month meetings of motor racing enthusiasts had to be discontinued. Now, in comparative peace, I put the appropriate notices in the press again and we continued with the meetings at St Stephen's Tavern.

I had the idea of compiling a register of all the people who could attend our meetings and, perhaps, starting similar gatherings at other centres in the Midlands and the North. However, nothing and no one was at all static, so we decided to continue the first-Saturday-of-the-month meetings in London and see how they developed.

More air raids – but not on London – including greater use of incendiary bombs on factories and airfields brought some changes in Britain's defence system. The Auxiliary Fire Service became the National Fire Service and our range of activities increased, enabling us to mobilize large forces to fight fires in other areas if needed.

In the watchroom.

Soon after Christmas, we had two more nights of heavy air raids, with oilbombs and large landmines. This time the attackers concentrated on the area around St Paul's Cathedral and the Guildhall. I feared that I might be recalled to full alert but, as these proved to be only isolated attacks, I remained on normal duty hours. On duty on the second night, I spent the whole time in the watchroom, moving pumps, water towers and water curtains with canvas dams to areas that lacked the required amount of water. Although both of those raids were heavy, they did not come on successive nights. The Fire Service was able to get all fires "in hand", so that they did not become beacons for later bombers. On the second night, 14 London firemen were killed and 250 more were injured, in addition to the large number of civilian casualties.

There followed some weeks without further raids. With good publicity from the motoring press, our unofficial enthusiasts' gatherings at St Stephen's Tavern grew in popularity. We raised funds for sending copies of *Motor Sport* to prisoner-of-war camps in Germany and we even received messages of thanks from some of the prisoners.

The Luftwaffe made one more attempt to destroy London by fire. On 10 and 11 May 1941, a vast number of bombers attacked London; thousands of incendiaries were dropped, followed by large numbers of high explosive bombs. The RAF did a magnificent job and a large percentage of German attackers was destroyed in the air. Although many fires were started, there was no real conflagration. Our fire-fighting techniques were so much improved, particularly by the mobile water supplies and better mustering of the crews. Fires did not spread as they had done in the attacks in the previous September and October. The Germans found that they could not burn London down. Apart from those two nights, all my nights on duty were spent peacefully, my uniform and equipment by the side of my bunk but, in fact, never again required.

At our flat in Warwick Road, New Barnet, we entertained many visitors from the world of motor racing, mostly men on leave from the Armed Services. Peter Robertson-Rodger, who owned Birkin Bentleys, came several times and brought his friend, Roddy Seys, who had a very nice open Bentley $4\frac{1}{2}$ with a light body. We three had some good times together until Roddy was tragically killed in a road accident. It so happened that most of our visitors came from the Navy and the RAF. One young Flying Officer, Derek Ousey, accompanied us to many parties and dances, but was reported missing after a raid and never found. These particular tragedies were the most distressing because, of course, the families went on hoping almost for ever.

St Stephen's Tavern was becoming overcrowded and some people asked if I could organize something similar out of London. I talked to Eric Giles, secretary of the Bugatti Owners' Club, because he attended all the St Stephen's Tavern meetings; he offered to help with any further administration. This was valuable because he had secretarial assistance at his office in Queen Street, off Curzon Street. I was getting a lot of encouragement. Sam Clutton said that his office would be available as well, so I began to think that we should extend our gatherings.

I was being pushed to organize something more ambitious. There was still a basic petrol ration but many people had extra coupons for special war work. Could I not organize a real motoring event some way out of London during a weekend? S H Capon was continuing to run a few meetings for the 750 MC, so I suggested to him that we could collaborate. The problem was to find somewhere just out of London. Someone suggested Chessington Zoo because there had been some Motor Club rallies there before the war. I telephoned the manager and arranged a visit: it seemed just right, so I discussed the project with Clutton, Anthony Heal and John Wyer. With their approval I contacted all the press and fixed a day: Saturday 13 July.

Penny and I decided that it was high time that we got married: it was no good waiting for the war to end, as it looked like going on for ever. We found a flat quite close to the Fire Station and Penny's Food Office. There was no garage, but the drive could accommodate a couple of cars. The nuptials were fixed for exactly a week after the Chessington Rally – you have to get your priorities well established in such matters!

Life was getting very hectic, because neither the war nor Heath, Booth & Co were stopping for my Enthusiasts' Meeting or my wedding. I was driving down to Brooklands nearly every day on a new project with Vickers. The circuit was heavily camouflaged. New factories were sprouting through the old bankings, so that it seemed unlikely that there would ever be motor racing there again – a very sad thought.

So, at Chessington Zoo on 13 July 1941 we had the first real wartime motoring rally. The press called it "The Enthusiasts' Rally". Nearly 200 attended, with a great selection of splendid cars. Many had saved up precious petrol rations for the occasion. Among the machines there was one of the ex-Malcolm Campbell V12 Sunbeam racing cars, together with his old 38/250 Mercedes which he had driven in the Irish Grand Prix and the Tourist Trophy. Anthony Heal brought his well-known 5-litre Ballot; Peter Monkhouse the 4-litre Darracq, one of the fastest sports car event machines at Brooklands. Peter and Ariel Clark came with the 1914 Grand Prix Mercedes and R G Sutherland brought a brand-new prototype Aston Martin, a streamlined saloon with the type name Atom.

Above
Chessington: Mark and Peter Monkhouse and Penny, with the Darracq and Ballot.

Above right:
Chessington: the Aston Martin Atom and other delectable cars.

Our world of motor racing was very well represented with John Bolster, Georges Roesch, Stuart Wilton, Charles Brackenbury, Eric Giles, Sam Clutton, Forrest Lycett, Michael May and Walter Norton and many other well-known personalities, as well as the Press – Bill Boddy, Laurence Pomeroy, Bunny Tubbs, H S Lindfield and Eric Findon.

Services duty rosters meant that not everyone was able to stay, but 160 people sat down to tea and George Monkhouse presented one of his splendid film shows.

I was delighted with the response and was inundated with requests to carry on organizing functions to keep the sport alive. We had been lucky, with perfect weather and the timing happened to be about right in that so much of the Army was around in Britain then.

Immediately after Chessington, I had to make preparations for my wedding to Penny the following weekend. Our furnished flat was almost ready. Three days before the nuptials, while taking a load of books and clothes to the flat, I slid a corner rather too enthusiastically, hit a kerb and turned the Austin Seven over on its side. Not a very good beginning – but I was alone, was not really injured and there was little real damage to the car. With help from a rather shocked bystander we righted the Austin before the police arrived. The local police who turned up were men I had already met through the Fire Service and they somewhat reluctantly agreed that there had not been an accident worth reporting. I was not injured: my bleeding chin must have been cut whilst shaving! The dirt and marks on the pavement were nothing, so I got away with it – just!

At the Fire Service, my good friends in the workshop soon righted the little wrongs in the Austin: a rather buckled wheel was straightened, a wing and running board mended and the whole thing tidied up in no time.

Exactly a week after Chessington, Penny and I were married at Holy Trinity Church, New Barnet, where Penny and all her family had always worshipped. Despite the wartime restrictions in every direction, and the fact that so many people were in the Forces, it was quite a large function. Most of our close family and many friends were able to be present. After the celebration, Penny's grandfather's chauffeur drove us away in a big Buick limousine. At my parents' home we changed mounts and set off in the little Austin Seven. In wartime Britain, of course, there was no thought of a glamorous honeymoon at an exotic venue.

Honeymoon: this was our bedroom! Penny with the spare wheel – we had a puncture.

We were glad and happy to get a week's leave to stay at an inn a little further away into the country. My basic petrol ration, plus useful additions from Peter Berthon and Richard Booth, took us to Braughing, 30 miles north of London. We also spent a couple of nights at Eastgate House with Raymond Mays and his mother, at Bourne another 40 miles on. After a nostalgic look at the ERA R4D, we returned to work.

At Chessington I had renewed my friendship with Peter Monkhouse and his wife, Elizabeth. Peter's partner, Ian Connell, was in the Army. Peter had turned the Monaco Motor and Engineering at Watford into a fine engineering shop, manufacturing parts for the Ministry of Aircraft Production; the firm was also the main subcontractor for British Oxygen, for whom it produced special valves.

I took Peter Berthon over to Monaco Motor to meet Peter Monkhouse. Our plants and capabilities were complementary and we were immediately able to increase our production of parts and assemblies.

My home in Barnet was ideally placed midway between Mortimer Engineering in London and Monaco at Watford. I bought another Austin Seven for myself, a 1934 two-seater, the "Army" model with hooks on the rear wheels – I think for towing a gun carriage. This was a good one, so Penny was able

Penny in the "Army" Austin Seven two-seater and our Labrador puppy, Soda.

to use the earlier fabric two-seater and my "Army" model was camouflaged in RAF style for visiting airfields.

When Churchill made Lord Beaverbrook Minister of Aircraft Production, Lord Brabazon became a leading light in LAP (London Aircraft Production), co-ordinating the production of aircraft engines, fuselage and parts over a wide area. AEC, of which "Brab" was a director, in peacetime the builders of London buses, played a prominent part and we became leading subcontractors at Mortimer Engineering and at Monaco.

CHAPTER FIVE

In many respects, things were going very well. I was always in touch with "Brab" and with his terrific drive and ability to get things done he achieved much. He was the terror of any timid civil servant who only worked by the book. "Brab" cut through red tape, feared no authority and was as straight as a die. On several occasions he told us, "We will do it first and seek permission afterwards: the war effort cannot wait for paperwork". I am sure he upset a few people, who feared his direct approach; but those who knew him loved him. From time to time, he gave me special jobs to do for him personally, reporting on projects and interviewing people with promising ideas.

We now came to the point when Peter Berthon insisted that I should work for him full-time. It was absurd that I should be on Fire Service duty, just waiting about. The Blitz on London was over, with very few bombs now and no big fires. At Heath, Booth & Co and at Mortimer Engineering we were being pressed for some very important jobs. One particular item was the manufacture of hinge brackets for the folding wings of Seafires, the Fleet Air Arm version of the Spitfire. "Brab" was interested in that job and told Berthon that it should have our first priority. It was getting behind schedule and Peter was getting practically no sleep. When, after two weeks working with Peter at Mortimer Engineering I was off for another week just standing by at the Fire Service in Barnet, Peter blew his top! He got an appointment at the Manpower Office to see if I could be released to work full-time for Mortimer.

Many forms were filled in and I attended meetings at the Ministry of Aircraft Production, the Admiralty and the London Fire Service Headquarters. The switch seemed possible, but until "Brab" intervened it was taking a lot of time. Then it all happened very quickly. I was released from the Fire Service and registered for military service in the Royal Naval Reserve, but was immediately loaned by the latter to industry and allocated to Mortimer Engineering. It all sounded very complicated. In effect, I was still on call if required for the Fire Service, as a part-time mobilizing officer. I believe I was the first person released to industry from the Fire Service in the London area.

Now I felt a different man and able to devote myself entirely to work with Peter Berthon. For many months we all worked at full speed. Berthon's capacity to do without sleep for a long time made life very difficult for the rest of the company, because when he did succumb after several days he would sleep during the day when the rest of us were at work. However, a great deal was done during those critical months. When the drawing office job eased, half of my time was chasing the work from our subcontractors and finding new outlets for our Admiralty and Ministry of Aircraft Production contracts. It was a hectic and exciting, but very enjoyable life; sometimes it included the use of Richard Booth's very good and rare Fiat 1500 coupé.

Britain had survived the London Blitz and equally heavy raids on other places like Coventry and Plymouth. It was now felt that an invasion of our shores stood less chance of success because our resources were improving all the time.

With the war moving into a more promising situation, life for me was very enjoyable. Visiting an Oxford airfield with Peter Monkhouse and Peter Berthon on some Vickers business, we arrived just as an air raid started. We were immediately pushed into a shelter but, after a few minutes, Berthon said that he needed to go back to the car to get some papers. The senior RAF officer in charge advised him not to do so; when Berthon insisted on going, he handed him a steel helmet. Typically, Berthon refused the headgear and strolled over to his car, collected his papers and stayed outside among the shrapnel and bombs watching the raid.

Two bombs landed on the airfield, one very close to the cars and hangar. Luckily, no one was injured. When it was all over, a very senior officer read the Riot Act to Berthon. Of course, it had no effect at all: both Monkhouse and I felt rather bad about it, but Berthon laughed it off. No one seemed able to worry Berthon and he certainly had no fear.

On two occasions during the blackout, I had to drive Berthon in one of the Aprilias. It was, of course, urgent business and we were very late with something. Peter sat in the back, reading and writing notes by torchlight. If I slowed down at all, Berthon would say, "Put your foot down, Rivers, you are hanging about". When I replied that it was too dark and I could not see, he said, "Just put your foot down; try hard". So I had to drive a lot faster than I really dared. At least, it was a darned sight safer than letting Peter drive. He really was a frightening driver and not all that good either. If Lord Howe specialized in near misses, Berthon went one better and usually managed to hit things.

Soon after the Chessington event, the basic petrol ration was considerably reduced. I felt that the next Enthusiasts' Meeting would have to be held in London. I went the rounds of the possible London hotels. We needed reasonable space for car parking, but also a central venue for public transport and I felt that a meeting with a Saturday lunch would probably be best. We required room for a film show as well. Since these events were not run by a club or an established organization, I needed to persuade a hotel to put it all on for me personally and I had to convince them that I could get the backing.

Mr U Bona, the manager of the Rembrandt Hotel, was most enthusiastic about the project and backed me to the hilt. So after the little meetings at St Stephen's Tavern and the function at Chessington Zoo, I decided on the Rembrandt Hotel for the first of the big London meetings on Saturday 5 October 1941. I had wonderful help from Sam Clutton, Eric Giles, Anthony Heal, Laurence Pomeroy and Bunny Tubbs, who handled the tickets. Again, George Monkhouse gave a film show; at the lunch the chair was taken by Raymond Mays. Louis Klementaski and George Monkhouse supplied a wonderful collection of big pictures, which decorated the hall.

This was another successful function and a pattern was establishing itself, in that everyone who was anyone in our world attended if it was at all possible. By popular demand, a second such event was booked. I continued to organize "Rembrandts", as they came to be called, regularly every two or three months throughout the rest of the war. There was no other activity uniting motor sport enthusiasts. I thought it proper to keep the RAC informed, but in fact no one there was interested.

Lord Howe wrote to me regularly from Glasgow urging me to carry on organizing events to keep people in touch after the first meeting. My wife, Penny, took on all the secretarial work of the "Rembrandts"; and I gathered a small advisory panel comprising Captain A W Phillips, A Percy Bradley, H J Morgan, Eric Giles, Anthony Heal and F G Craner. I felt that this panel would give the organization more credibility.

At Heath, Booth & Co we were involved with parts for amphibious tanks. The overriding problem was the inevitable great weight of any sort of tank. An early official demonstration in front of military top brass proved a disaster, as the tank rumbled across the land, down a slope into a lake and immediately sank to the bottom! The crew bobbed up to the surface and swam ashore. Someone, as it were, forgot to put the plug in. It was all rather like another official demonstration, this time of a new seaplane, when a high-ranking RAF officer was invited to step off the aircraft into a waiting barge; he stepped off on the wrong side and went straight into the water! He, too, had to swim ashore.

Peter Berthon had an idea involving motorcycles for military use. I cannot now remember what the scheme was. He instructed me to get hold of a big, fast motorcycle straight away. Of course, no new motorcycles were available to civilians then, so I set off round the agents in the Great Portland Street area of London. I found a 1000 cc Square Four Ariel and it was delivered to our works.

Peter Berthon and Richard Booth gazed at it with admiration. Then Peter said, "Well, Rivers, you bought it – now give us a demonstration". I told them that I was not really a motorcyclist and could only with difficulty ride one at all. Nevertheless, they insisted that I should start it up and ride it up and down the road. I was not at all keen: it was so heavy and I had only had a few rides some years ago on a friend's much lighter machine. Anyhow, I had to have a go, but was a bit wobbly and very slow. Then Peter said, "Go off again, but when you are level with us just give it a bit of a burst of throttle in second gear"

Once again, I did not really like the idea at all, but thought that it would be all right if I gave it just one "blip" with the twist-grip of the throttle.

I was going quite slowly and smoothly and was getting more confident. When I drew level with Peter and Richard, I looked towards them as I twisted the grip, opening the throttle. The machine leaped forward, standing on its rear wheel, with me hanging on for dear life; I had the greatest difficulty in closing the throttle as I shot backwards. Peter and Richard were most amused and begged me to do it again.

Not me! From then on, Peter Berthon took over the Ariel and obviously liked it. Peter's motorcycle scheme never came to anything, but sometimes he enjoyed riding it to work if the weather was fine. On several occasions, I had to ride it home in the wet while Peter drove one of the Lancias. I did not take to the bike at all, but I suppose it was all right in good weather. I always rode it very slowly, because it frightened me. I am sure Peter was right when he told me that such a heavy bike was only a proposition at a reasonable speed, but I was scared.

I bought yet another Austin Seven, again a 1934 model, but this was the Arrow Sports four-seater, a rare model but very attractive – I thought of it as a sort of poor man's HRG. We sold the 1927 fabric two-seater that Penny had been using and swapped around between the "Army" Seven and the Arrow.

During that period of the war, the talking point was always invasion. Every day, every week, we were warned of the imminent German invasion of Britain. Airborne troops and landings by parachute were expected, preceding a seaborne invasion on the south or east coast.

Peter Berthon leaving "Noddings" on the Ariel, with Charles Follett in shorts.

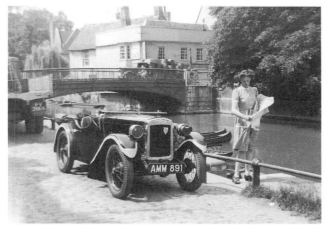

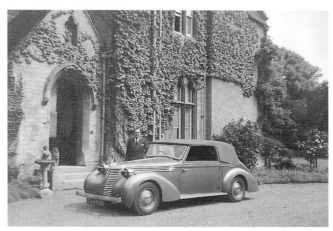

Above left:
Penny with the Arrow at Cambridge (a "poor man's HRG"). Note ERA and Brooklands Club badges and wartime livery.

Above right:
Richard Booth with the rare 1½-litre Fiat.

The Home Guard was a real part of our home defence. It was indeed a "Dad's Army" as portrayed on television, never actually confronting an invasion; nevertheless it was there and always on the ready. It is difficult to assess the mood of a whole nation, but I believe that the fairly long middle period after Dunkirk, but before the Americans came into the war, was a good time. We were alone and rather proud of it. Fearful but not too fearful, having a strange faith that we were in the right and that right would somehow or other prevail.

There was great pride in the spectacular feats of the young

pilots of the RAF. Most of us need to have heroes and there were plenty at hand; those middle years of the war were Britain's best. There is nothing like the satisfaction of knowing that you are doing the right thing. For most of us it does not happen very often; but I think that, at that time, the whole country basked in the glow of a certain amount of fairly well-justified satisfaction. That did much to alleviate the tremendous problems of those days.

When my work on some Admiralty contracts was completed, I was seconded to Peter Monkhouse's Monaco Works to help on MAP contracts for a day or two each week. There was excellent rapport between Peter Berthon and Peter Monkhouse, both rather the same sort of engineers, inclined to push ahead with new and untried experimental ideas despite what more cautious voices might say.

Peter Monkhouse desperately needed a production controller at his factory and he asked me if I would take the job on if Peter Berthon would release me. This was a reasonable proposition because of the change of work by the two companies. A request was made to the Manpower Board again; with backing from Lord Brabazon, I joined Peter Monkhouse as Production Controller and Commercial Manager of the Monaco Works. I was still on loan from the RNR, where I had been listed as a sub-lieutenant, given a number and told that I would be notified if required.

I was so lucky that my work still had a motor racing connection and I was given full co-operation with the organization of the "Rembrandts". I found my new job with Monkhouse much harder; but it was probably good for me that I was made to carry out a lot of tasks that I did not really like. I found myself responsible for the company's workload, ordering all the material and accepting contracts that kept our machine shop full day and night. I found this very worrying.

I did not take to the detail work, but we had an excellent chief draughtsman in Bertram Sharp, who shared our motor sport enthusiasm and had already done a lot of design work on racing cars before the war. Our chief inspector, Tony Rumfitt, also had a special interest in motor sport and trials cars.

My close friendship with Peter developed – and we shared the same sort of humour, which always helped. Our wives got on very well, so our families spent a lot of time together.

When I had been at ERA our social activities were mostly within the circle of close friends of Raymond Mays, Lord Howe and Humphrey Cook. Now the circle had widened, but the London theatre parties started again and Penny and I often joined Raymond Mays, Peter Berthon and his wife, Lorna. The Ivor Novello musicals were our favourites, always followed by going round to meet the stars in their dressing rooms and late supper parties afterwards.

Penny, Peter Monkhouse and his wife, "Bumpy".

The occasional air raid sent all of us down to the cellars, except Peter Berthon, who was always completely oblivious of danger. I remember that on one such occasion, when there was a sudden and quite heavy air raid at about midnight, Ray and I sheltered at the entrance of Grosvenor House while Peter, hatless, insisted on walking across Hyde Park to see what was going on.

There was a lot of shrapnel falling about but, of course, he took no notice.

This reminded me of how Peter, many years before, had ridden on the wall of death at Skegness in a sidecar with a grown lion! Neither Ray nor I was prepared to go on the wall at all.

At the Monaco Works the motor side was almost dormant, only the sale of Pool petrol and oil at our filling station remaining active. Nevertheless, our own road cars were properly serviced and our chief racing mechanic, Jack Jaguard, was sometimes fished out from aircraft production problems to deal with a sports car. Of course, there were no car sales, but Peter Monkhouse managed to acquire a fine Bugatti Type 55, which we sometimes used with trade numberplates.

On just one occasion, we had the use of a Monza Alfa Romeo from John James as well – the car I had already driven on test at Brooklands with Luis Fontes. Peter and I had a splendid run, Peter driving the Type 55 and I the Monza. We had a dice on open roads and, from time to time, we swapped cars. I think it did us a power of good and I am sure we were the better for it. Endless discussions between us on the relative merits of the Bugatti and Alfa always ended with Peter preferring the "Bug" and me the Alfa – both models were prime examples in fine condition. I wonder, which would you prefer?

Above left:
At the Monaco Works: John James' Alfa Romeo Monza, a car the author had driven with Luis Fontes before the war.

Above right:
At a 750 MC Club meeting on the Great West Road: Peter Monkhouse, Bumpy, Mark and Penny with the trade-plated Type 55 Bugatti.

Although my work with Monkhouse at Monaco was harder and more difficult than my previous job, it was less rushed and there was more time to organize the "Rembrandts". Each meeting had a different theme, but all were concerned with racing and as the war news got better and peace was on the horizon, we talked about and planned the future of the sport.

PART II

KEEPING THE SPORT ALIVE

*Work with Peter Monkhouse
at Monaco's at Watford and
the organization of the
"Rembrandts," keeping the sport
alive during the war*

CHAPTER SIX

In the summer of 1943, I planned a more or less outdoor meeting at the London Zoo instead of a normal "Rembrandt". A reasonable attendance resulted and, once again, we were able to see some interesting cars – Sir Antony Stamer's 1750 Alfa Romeo; Terry Breen with a boat-tail 3-litre Bentley; together with his partner, Alec Park, with a Lancia Lambda. Motor racing personalities all the way from Australia were Joan Richmond and Robert Waddy. Then we returned to normal "Rembrandts" at the hotel, which continued to be increasingly popular.

A friend of mine, who had been a keen member of the ERA Club, was Donald McCullough. During the war he became famous as the question master of the BBC Brains Trust programme, so I thought it would be a good idea to have a Brains Trust of our own at a "Rembrandt". The "brains" were Laurence Pomeroy, Peter Monkhouse, Leslie Ballamy, Sam Clutton, Peter Berthon, and the MG driver, Fred Thatcher. Fred had raced an N-type MG Magnette and had a very attractive actress sister called Heather; she had ridden with me for a couple of laps on the Outer Circuit at Brooklands. Now like many famous actors and actresses she was with ENSA entertaining the troops. Of course, I invited Donald McCullough to be our question master. The Brains Trust was so popular that I organized more of them. Later question masters were Sam Clutton and Rodney Walkerley: other "brains" included Captain Phillips of the RAC; Raymond Mays; Louis Klementaski; Percy Bradley, Clerk of the Course at Brooklands; Fred Craner from Donington; John Morgan of the JCC; Eric Giles; Anthony Heal; John Bolster; Roy Nockolds, the artist; plus that always controversial personality, Georges Roesch.

It seemed to me that we should start to consider what sort of sports cars should be made after the war. I therefore got a panel of designers and other experts to start this as a talking point at another "Rembrandt". Cecil Kimber, Robert Waddy, Laurence Pomeroy, H R Godfrey, E C Gordon England and Donald Bastow all put forward interesting and varied ideas for the future.

At another "Rembrandt", drivers such as Oliver Bertram, Kay

Petre, Raymond Mays and Peter Clark talked from the point of view of the conductors.

The organization of races and other events was discussed by Harry Edwards of the BRDC, Johnny Morgan of the JCC, "Jackie" Masters MCC, Percy Bradley BARC, and Fred Craner. Captain George Eyston was in the chair. Another chairman was Lord Brabazon of Tara, whom we had all known at Brooklands as Colonel J T C Moore-Brabazon.

Peter Monkhouse and I had an exciting time visiting a tank testing ground. Rupert Instone, the Shelsley Special driver, was in charge and he took us for a very exciting run in a Cromwell tank. There was only room inside for Rupert and Peter, so I had to cling on outside on top. I reckoned that Rupert got enthusiastic about showing how he could fling the Cromwell about and forgot that I was hanging on by the skin of my teeth. I only just managed it, but all the time feared that I would be thrown off and crushed in the greasy slime by our Cromwell or one of the other tanks.

Having used Austin Sevens for nearly all my private motoring during the war, I thought in 1943 that the outlook was sufficiently promising to warrant laying down a more interesting car for use later. I decided it should be something of vintage character, up to about 2 litres in capacity, sufficiently tough to tow a trailer with a racing car, but with good all-weather equipment and ample accommodation for two or three and their luggage.

The choice seemed to lie between a 12/50 or 12/60 Alvis and a 2-litre Lagonda. Finally we felt that the Alvis would be preferable to the Lagonda, partly because nearly all the old Lagondas had fabric bodies. I contacted a rabid Alvis enthusiast called John Cooper, who ran an amateur équipe called Scuderia Impecuniosa. John confirmed my opinions and told me the probable snags. It seemed that the ideal car for me would be a 1932 Alvis TL model: this was the last in that series. I thought the best plan would be to buy one in rough condition and have it reconditioned, as I was in a good position to do this with Monaco Motor & Engineering Co.

I failed to find a TL, but eventually located a 1931 TK "beetle-back" two-seater. Its deficiencies as compared with the TL were that it had bolt-on wheels, no water temperature gauge and no rev counter; otherwise the models were identical.

A friend of mine towed the rather battered Alvis home and the work of reconstruction was begun: there was no hurry nor, as yet, any sign of a reasonable petrol allowance. We decided to do the reconstruction in three main sections. Brian Ashworth, a good engineer with a 3-litre Bentley, who had a small works near Enfield, rebuilt the chassis; we rebuilt the engine at our own Monaco Works; and I knew a coachbuilder in London who would do the body. The block was sleeved by Laystalls and the crankshaft reground.

I renewed contact with the Alvis Company in Coventry, in particular Mr Smith-Clarke, William Dunn and A F Varney, whom I had got to know when we were involved with an Alvis for the Tourist Trophy race before the war. They were in the new aero-engine works. Willie Dunn showed me the remains of

The 1931 TK Alvis; Penny at the wheel.

the old car works, which had been completely destroyed in the Coventry blitz. Destroyed it was, but somehow or other some production was carried on in the remnants of the factory.

I was taken on a tour round Coventry, a shocking sight. More devastation in one night than we ever had in London – and the concentration of destruction in time and place must have been terrible, very different from the horror of the London Blitz, which we had had time to get used to.

I asked if Alvis had plans for a postwar car. They said there were plans, but would not give me any details. However, they were most helpful, giving me the various parts I needed for my 12/60.

Various small modifications were made to the original body design. At that time there was no fetish about originality and I personally have always liked modifications of my own design if they were not out of character or period. The old Alvis seats with rather hard squabs were scrapped in favour of more comfortable ones taken from an Austin; and the driving seat was mounted 2.5 inches higher than the passenger's to give more visibility. The heavy metal dicky seat lid was discarded in favour of a tonneau cover and a new aircraft-type collapsible dicky seat was fitted.

The headlamp tie bar was moved further forward and smaller diameter headlamps were fitted in the centre, in the Alpine Talbot style out of love for that model! An extra tie-bar was fitted between the dumb irons so that the extended starting handle could be fitted through it, enabling the engine to be swung without barking the knuckles.

In the interests of economy, I used a single updraught 30 mm Solex carburettor, supplied by my friend John Wyer, the Solex London Manager. We fitted an SU petrol pump instead of the original Petrolift. I liked this Alvis very much indeed and it was the answer for me at that time: the marque and the company were close to my heart.

My friend Peter Monkhouse was in a position to go a good deal better. At that time, the Bugatti Owners' Club decided to sell the Type 51 that Ettore Bugatti had presented to the Club in 1939. Although it was a wonderful gift, it proved to be rather a white elephant, as it was so difficult to decide who should drive it. Obviously the people with the requisite amount of experience already had suitable cars of their own. There were clear difficulties in handing over such a potent and expensive piece of machinery to any one inexperienced. No doubt, the BOC council must have been loath to part with the car, but the war was still on and there did not seem much prospect of racing for a long time, so the Type 51 became available.

Peter did a deal with Eric Giles and, on Easter Monday in April 1943, Peter and I travelled down to the Giles' home in Surrey by train. We brought with us a pair of trade plates and a roll of 4-inch wide canvas. Eric promised to fasten a batten across the tail so that we could stretch the canvas to make some sort of impromptu "wings" to comply with the law. We also brought with us a bulb horn from a child's bicycle, but we doubted if it would be heard above the roar of the unsilenced Bugatti engine.

The Type 51 had been filled with racing fuel on the outbreak of war. This had tended to separate out, so we drained the fuel, shook it up and refilled the tank before setting off on a 6-mile detour around London. It was a fantastic journey. Peter drove nearly all the way, although I had a short spell at the wheel. We

The BOC Type 51 Bugatti.

were cheered on by numerous military convoys, who were no doubt surprised to see and hear a Grand Prix car being driven in such a manner in such a place.

We came across several policemen, but they obviously did not believe their eyes or ears, so we were well past them before anyone could do anything about it. At one roundabout, near Beaconsfield, a military policeman gave us the thumbs up signal and beckoned us to do just one more circuit of the roundabout for his pleasure. Peter was driving and gave him the works: second gear with plenty of wheelspin and all the resultant tail wagging and pleasant odour. Back at the works, the Type 51 was put away for the time being.

CHAPTER SEVEN

"Noddings": Penny in the willow garden by the pond.

Penny and I, looking forward to the time when we might start a family of our own, were very pleased when Penny's mother found for us a delightful little cottagey house. It was quite close to "Rothiemay", the large Victorian house that she had shared with her parents – Penny's grandparents, Mr and Mrs John Long. This, our first house, we called "Noddings", which seemed to suit it. It was detached, but close to other rather similar houses, in a quiet road about half a mile from the Great North Road. Although "Noddings" was quite small, it had a charming garden, with a willow, a pond, plenty of other trees and a good brick garage, together with a covered side way that could easily house a second car. We moved in and allocated one bedroom to be a nursery, long before there was any sign of impending children.

As well as going to most of the musical comedies in London, we were certainly at all of the intimate revues starring the two Hermiones, Baddeley and Gingold. "Totie" Baddeley was a great friend of Raymond Mays and we had some most amusing parties in her flat over No. 100 Piccadilly. Her first husband had been the Hon. David Tennant, a great motor racing enthusiast who had owned one of the Special 7-litre Straight Eight Leylands. Hermione Baddeley's stories of her rides in the Leyland on Brooklands track suggested that David Tennant's driving was nearly as mad as Peter Berthon's – but not quite as mad as when Peter had driven Hermione from a party at Maidenhead to get her to the stage door of the Ambassador's Theatre, when somebody's watch had stopped and it looked as though Hermione would miss her first entrance in her show. They made it – just!

I saw more of Jack Hulbert, his brother Claude and his brother-in-law Peter Haddon. When we had been filming at Elstree before the war, I never succeeded in getting them interested in cars or motor racing; when they tried to drive the Bentleys I took to the studios, they all made dreadful noises with the gears. Sometimes they had to be pushed on to the set and even towed off!

Bobby Howes had the same difficulty at first, but he persevered and eventually got the knack of double declutching and bought an Alvis sports car for himself. Now, meeting him again, he quite enjoyed a drive in my 12/60 Alvis, but said that he preferred his own 12/70, which had a synchromesh gearbox.

Another motor racing enthusiast from the stage who came to the "Rembrandts" was Elsie and Doris Waters' brother, Jack Warner. He had been a member of Charles Follett's Alvis team in rallies, later becoming famous as "PC 49" in the BBC radio series "Dixon of Dock Green". Jack was a great fan of Raymond Mays and even talked of buying an ERA. I put him in touch with Reg Parnell, who had several available, but nothing came of it.

To set the very strange scene of that time, here are some typical prices asked for used sports and racing cars: Frazer Nash, 1½-litre supercharged sprint car "Spook", £290; Bentley Speed Six, VOP Tourer, £215; Bentley, the actual Thistlethwaite Le Mans 3-litre car, £350; Alvis 12/50 two-seater, £105; Talbot 90, Tourer, £75; Bugatti Type 44, chassis complete, £145; Bentley, MG J2 Type, Midget, £70; Austin Seven Nippy Sports two-seater, £75.

Charles Follett and his family lived in a rambling old house just up the road from "Noddings" – our gardens were only separated by a lane. We saw a lot of Charles, his wife, Pearl, his three pretty daughters and young son, Paul. Previously, the Folletts had lived at Hadley Wood in the same county, only six miles away.

With so many British servicemen stationed in this country and the "Rembrandts" the only motor racing venue, we had many visitors at "Noddings", and to the Folletts. Among the regular visitors were Lieutenant Marcus Chambers, Jack Warner, Ian Nichols, Lord Waleran, Cecil Kimber, George Monkhouse, Laurence Pomeroy, George Eyston; and, of course, the Bourne contingent, Ray, Peter and Lorna and Peter Monkhouse and his wife. If the weather was fine, Peter brought the Type 51 Bugatti, which always created the right atmosphere. An occasional visitor was a rather shy and quiet young man called Roy Salvadori, looking and sounding very English, with a London voice, despite his Italian name. He was buying an ex-Dobbs 2-litre Riley. He told me that he and his brother Sidney were in the Trade, but neither of them had driven anything very fast – he wondered if he would be able to manage it.

Ray often met Ivor Novello and Phyllis and Zena Dare, who starred in Novello musicals; so I soon got to know more of the stars I had first seen on the stage when I was a schoolboy.

After our theatre parties, we usually finished up at the Music Box, an intimate little club where nearly all the members were on the stage. We soon got to know the resident pianist, Hugh Wade, who could play and sing absolutely anything that had ever been played in a show. One night at the Music Box, talking with Phyllis Dare, I told her that the first musical I ever saw was "Lido Lady", where she played opposite Jack Hulbert and they sang a charming duet called "Here In My Arms". I told Phyllis that I had bought the gramophone record and throughout my schooldays, in my dreams, I had imagined myself singing that song with her in my arms. Phyllis said, "Come on, let's make the dreams come true; let's sing it together quietly to one another". Hugh Wade remembered the tune: I had no voice at all, but just together in the corner, with the beautiful Phyllis Dare in my arms, it really was a dream come true!

The stage connection became much closer with the opening in London of the Stage Door Canteen. This was the British version of a splendid entertainment canteen for rank and file servicemen, under the auspices of the American Theater Wing War Service Inc. The location was a famous London landmark, "The Pop", in Piccadilly. A lifelong friend of mine, Harold Thackrah, was the Entertainment Director and I was roped in to help. "Tubby" Thackrah's job was to provide a nightly show, seven days a week. All the artistes gave their performances free and the show took place quite late each night, after the last performance in the ordinary London theatres.

The magnitude of his work may be judged by the fact that more than a thousand artistes performed at Stage Door Canteen during the first six months. We had a permanent band for dancing and an average of 750 meals a night was served in the cafeteria in the basement beneath the dance floor and stage. Using my 12/60 Alvis, I often had to pick up artistes from theatre stage doors at the end of their shows, race them to Stage Door Canteen, and then take them back to their homes late at night. I soon got to know all the West End theatre managements. Vivian van Damm, running the Windmill, introduced me to his daughter Sheila, who was helping him and we became friends in the world of theatre long before she became famous as a rally driver.

Stage Door Canteen was a tremendous success. All the great stars of those days, including Bea Lillie, Elizabeth Welch, Phyllis

Stage door canteen programme.

Above left:
Stage door canteen: the green room with Sonia, the secretary, at her desk.

Above right:
The stage connection: with Jack Hulbert's daughter at the Rembrandt Hotel.

Calvert, Ciceley Courtneidge, Marlene Dietrich, Noel Coward, Jack Buchanan, Bing Crosby and Fred Astaire, appeared there.

There was a predominance of males at Stage Door Canteen, mostly American GIs, so we always provided a galaxy of attractive hostesses, usually from the choruses of the current musicals. My job was finding and collecting these girls. I like to think that rides in my open sports Alvis and stories of

Brooklands helped to encourage them to become enthusiasts for the sport after the war.

Hermione Baddeley's very attractive young daughter, Pauline Tennant, was going on the stage herself and her manager was Jack Dunfee, so I saw quite a lot of them. It seemed that, at every step I took, the motor racing connection appeared. Jack Hulbert's daughter came to one of my "Rembrandts" and Laurence Pomeroy was marrying a stunningly beautiful actress, Elsa Tee, who was in rehearsal for a musical with Bobby Howes and Jack Hulbert.

During the latter part of the war, the only real danger in the London area came from the V1 and V2 missiles. We became a little blasé about the original V1 flying bombs because we could hear them coming. Many fell in London. When a close one shut off its engine, you just dived for shelter under anything at hand until it exploded. I was having lunch alone upstairs in a restaurant in Soho one day and I was sitting opposite a very pretty girl. I got to know her very quickly and rather intimately as we crouched together, both of us inside my duffle coat under that little table, as a V1 landed just down the road.

The later V2 rockets were a real menace; they were silent so the only thing you could do was to ignore them. We were rather fortunate: one Saturday, Penny and I went out to lunch at a restaurant in Finchley, about three miles away. When we came home we saw that a V2 had landed on a house close by, completely demolishing it, killing several people and damaging many more houses. All our south-facing windows were blown in and long pieces of broken glass were embedded in the wall over

The Alvis 12/60 renovated: note the tonneau over the dicky seat.

the chair where I normally sat. Apart from these broken windows and some roof tiles, no harm was done to us, as nobody was in the house at the time.

My 12/60 Alvis was finished in black with blue upholstery and silver wheels: I was very pleased with the result. "Why wasn't it blue?" people ask me now. However, it is an odd fact that nearly all cars at that time were black and very few people considered having a light colour. It seemed natural to me to have my Alvis like Raymond Mays' ERA and his road cars. The Alvis was my everyday transport and, although there was no competition motoring, I was at least driving the right sort of car again.

With all the pre-war motor clubs inactive for several years, it was perhaps not surprising that some young enthusiasts started

Above left:
Monaco Motor and Engineering Co. Ltd, Watford, in wartime.

Above right:
At another 750 MC meeting: on display, the ex-Craig Bugatti Type 59.

new ones. Of course, there were no active events, but the new clubs ran a lot of social meetings. One near to me, the North London Enthusiasts' Car Club, under its very energetic secretary, George Bance, grew at a great rate and prospered in every direction. I had been asked to advise on administration and became its chairman. I brought in S C H Davis, Sir Malcolm Campbell, W M Couper (the well-known Talbot driver), Raymond Mays and Peter Berthon to give talks to the club. Enthusiasts' car clubs sprang up in the Midlands and the North of England, all indicating a splendidly increasing interest in the sport.

One slight problem arose in that a few of the new enthusiasts, not realizing the standing of the old pre-war clubs, did try to suggest that the new men and the new clubs should have a much larger say in the future of motor sport than would have been desirable. However, those of us who had been involved with the sport for many years managed to moderate their enthusiasm and, with good guidance from our technical press, this never became too much of a problem.

With the running down of war contracts, the motor industry gradually returned to a little of its own old activities – but, oh, so slowly. Our old garage business opened up and we started to prepare sports and racing cars for the future. The Bugatti Owners' Club Type 51 Bugatti was soon on the road and we were also working on the ex-Malcolm Campbell Mercedes and an SSK model for John James. A special single-seater MG K3 Magnette, started before the war for Hamish Weir, was being completed. A strange thing about nearly all car designers is that they have a special idiosyncrasy, a fetish almost. In the case of Peter Monkhouse, he always wanted a very short chassis. His plan for Weir's Magnette was to shorten it by more than 1 ft; with some difficulty he was persuaded to reduce it by only 9 in.

Much lighter cross-members were fitted. The engine was fitted much lower in the frame; its Roots-type supercharger blew at 12 lb and it developed 110 bhp at 6400 rpm. We used the normal ENV preselector gearbox, but the drive was taken to a special double reduction rear-axle assembly. This enabled the propeller shaft to be lowered by 4 in. This new arrangement made it possible to have the driver sitting very low down in the centre of the car, with his right foot operating the brake and throttle and his left foot, on the other side of the gearbox, operating the clutch. Lockheed provided splendid hydraulic brakes; and, with a universally jointed column, there was a central steering position.

A great attempt was made to reduce the weight by employing Elektron sheet for the bulkheads, instrument panel and many tubes used in the body, which was constructed of 18 SWG aluminium. It was planned to use this car for long-distance events, so a 40 gal tank was fitted – but it only weighed 40 lb. I was looking forward to testing this monoposto Magnette.

At the Monaco works in Watford, Peter Monkhouse was convinced that we should be in the aero-engine business after the war, believing that there would be a tremendous increase in private flying. He was determined to be in the vanguard of the rush to produce light aero-engines. I therefore took him to see Lord Brabazon, who was of course full of praise for Peter's determination, but fearful of the cost and time it would take for

The Monaco MG K3.

us to get a new engine in production, particularly as we were new in that field.

However, Peter was full of enthusiasm and already knew an engine designer in whom he had complete confidence. Ian Connell, still joint managing director of Monaco but in the Army, was not keen on the aero-engine project and wrote to say that he himself would like to continue with the old motor business. Peter therefore decided that he would start another, separate business to produce the aero-engine and would remain a director, but not joint managing director, of the motor business. A new factory was already under construction and available in the nearby village of Kings Langley, so Peter formed the new company, Monaco Engines Limited. I continued with Peter as his commercial manager and production controller and we completed the building of the factory at Kings Langley.

So far as real work was concerned, both Peter and I were fully occupied at the new engine factory; but for play – which I think occupied quite a bit of time! – we were often at the old premises at Watford with the racing cars.

We started testing sports and racing cars on the road again. The Watford and Barnet bypasses were still very deserted and in good condition. We used trade plates and, with stripped racing cars, we usually made some attempts to fit token wings and silencers. The police were very tolerant about such things. With my pre-war experience as a consultant to the Vice Squad at Scotland Yard and with good friends at the Police School at

Duke Woolley at the wheel with Peter Monkhouse in the MG TB for the 1939 TT.

Hendon, I had learned a lot about police proceedings. In those days, as well as over the years, I have always found the British police very co-operative, very much on our side. I have seen so many people foolishly on the defensive, or even antagonistic, when stopped by the police. The police standard of driving has certainly always been a lot higher than the norm; even in the immediate postwar period before the Hendon School was fully operative, their general technical knowledge was of course very considerable. I had a good friend, S J Humphreys, who was in charge of all the squad cars at Scotland Yard.

Monaco produced a special MG TB model for Duke Woolley for the 1939 Tourist Trophy, which had had to be abandoned because of the outbreak of war. The engine changes included an increase in bore to 70 mm, giving a swept-volume of 1385 cc. New gears were cut for the close-ratio box and a new exhaust system was fitted, as was an entirely new body of very light alloy with a shaped tail containing the fuel tank. The total weight was only 1512 lb. Peter's idea of low-mounted headlamps faired in with the body gave a considerable reduction in frontal area: at 5000 rpm, the car achieved 90 mph very quickly indeed.

We did some more development on this car and decided that we would market the model as a Monaco TT Type, on the new TC-type chassis that was being produced at Abingdon. Duke

Woolley agreed that we should use this car ourselves for development until he was demobilized from the services and I did a considerable mileage in it.

Monaco's racing shop was full of exciting machinery. L G Johnson, whom I had known before the war with a BMW Type 328, came over and bought Ian Connell's Darracq, the car that Arthur Dobson drove in the "Fastest Sports Car" race at Brooklands. Alan Best bought the lovely Bugatti Type 55, which

Peter Monkhouse with the left-hand-drive Mercedes SSK.

Peter and I had been using. John James was undoubtedly our best customer, as he was acquiring a wonderful selection of racing cars. Apart from the ex-Malcolm Campbell 38/250 Mercedes, he bought from Powys-Lybbe the famous ex-Brian Lewis Monza Alfa Romeo. His most exciting purchase comprised the two ex-Malcolm Campbell 4-litre Sunbeams, which had been known as "Tiger" and "Tigress" when raced by Kaye Don.

Of course, Peter and I tested these cars on the road whenever possible and great fun it was too. On one occasion, we were out on the Denham bypass with the Weir MG K3, the 38/250 Mercedes and the Type 51 Bugatti. Believe it or not, the police were with us as well, with one of their official Wolseleys. We used a fairly long straight, which culminated in a fast uphill left-hand bend. Peter was driving the Mercedes and, at the end of the fast straight, he had to lift off to take the fast bend, in case there was anything just out of sight. The police sergeant suggested that he should drive up to the fast corner and signal us if it was clear, so that Peter could have a real go: which he did, cornering at 110 mph. The sergeant congratulated him and, when we were packing up to go back to the works, reminded us that we had forgotten to put the trade plates on the Bugatti on our run out. He said that we should put them on to make certain that it was really legal. We certainly had every co-operation from the police. I suppose it just could not happen today – the more's the pity.

The basic design of the new aero-engine was completed, but Peter was getting bogged down with difficulties building the prototype, getting licences and special permits for materials and also coping with a lot of paperwork from the Air Ministry. At a lunch with Lord Brabazon, I told him of the difficulties and he said that he knew two young men at the Ministry who would be very helpful – Peter Masefield and Rodwell Banks. "Brab" telephoned Masefield and made an appointment for us.

This meeting proved to be the answer to our immediate problems. Masefield and Banks smoothed the way in many directions. The latter even came over to Kings Langley and helped with some of the technical problems. He and Peter Masefield gave much needed encouragement to Peter Monkhouse and introduced us to the manufacturers of a new light aircraft, the Chrislea Ace. They were looking for just the sort of engine we were building. This led to very promising meetings and a future plan to promote the Chrislea Ace jointly. It was hoped that one day we would move the Monaco engine works to Honiton, near Exeter, close to where the Ace was being built. I had little to do with this project itself, being only required to keep our business occupied with other subcontract work. This I was able to do, again largely through "Brab", with the London Aircraft Production Company.

Chrislea catalogue.

OVER TO YOU –

THE CHRISLEA AIRCRAFT COMPANY LIMITED, ENGLAND.

CHAPTER EIGHT

There was one more "Rembrandt" meeting, at which, very appropriately, Earl Howe took the chair. Now it only remained to hand over the reins to the proper motor clubs to get real racing going again.

Now that the war was going well and it was thought that it could not last much longer, the film industry was enlarging its scope. I reminded MGM of the service I had given before the war as the company's motoring and motor racing consultant, supplying cars and sometimes driving them. Now some work of that sort came my way again and at the Monaco works we made good use of the Bugatti, plus a couple of MGs.

On location at Elstree I drove a fine Lagonda that Judy Campbell was using in a film called *The World Owes Me a Living*. At Pinewood, I spent a whole week racing up and down the set in the Monaco MG TB. My father, more or less retired from the London Stock Exchange, came with me for a couple of days, just for the fun of it. He was fascinated to see it all, met some of the stars and enjoyed the refreshments provided in the big canteen. At the end of the week, I was going through my charges and expenses with the producer. He had been very pleased with the MG and, when he agreed my fee, he said "What about your mechanic who was with you for two of the days – if we pay him 25 per cent of your fee, would that be OK?" Very surprised, I hurriedly agreed, in case he asked any questions. He obviously never realized that my father had been only an interested spectator. I reckoned that my dear father, in his casual clothes certainly, but wearing a bowtie and his monocle, did not really look like a mechanic and certainly had no knowledge of how the engine worked. When I gave him his fee earned as a "racing mechanic" at the film studio, he was most amused and his story was soon around the Stock Exchange.

On 7 March 1945 our first child, Peter, was born at a nursing home close to Cockfosters. The birth was heralded by a V2 rocket which landed rather uncomfortably close to the building,

The final "Rembrandt" meeting. At the top table, left to right: Leslie Johnson, Penny, the author, Earl Howe, the Countess Howe, Raymond Mays, Marquess Campden, Maurice Olley, John Dugdale, Mrs Mayne, Philip Mayne, John Hugenholtz, Eva Meisl. In the foreground: Henry Coy, "Pingo" Lester, Jack Bartlett, Peter Monkhouse, Peter Berthon, Sam Gilby and Peggy Candy.

but nobody was hurt. My younger brother Peter, a glider pilot, had been engaged in the very hazardous operation at Arnhem. When we learned that he was again on another planned airborne operation, we were desperately fearful for him. It was partly in thankfulness for his safe return that we had our son christened Peter. However, it was also for my two friends, Peter Berthon and Peter Monkhouse, with whom I was working at that time. So no other name could have been chosen. His first drives, still unborn, on the way to the nursing home and in Penny's arms on his return, were in my 12/60 Alvis – we made certain that he had the right start!

We modified the accommodation in the Alvis, arranging for a carrycot to be fitted behind the front seats under an extension of the hood. This was a worthwhile improvement, which enabled us to take Peter with us to many meetings.

Cecil Kimber, who had founded the MG Company and was its guiding star in the pre-war years, had been cruelly dismissed by the Nuffield Organization when engaged on a wartime aircraft contract. He had joined the Specialloid Pistons company. Now, with his second wife Gillie, he had moved to a charming little house, "Rose Cottage", just around the corner from us. So, with Charles Follett on our doorstep and "Kim" so close, we all spent quite a lot of time together. Once again, there was a theatre connection. Kim was a friend of Bud Flannagan and I was a friend of Jimmy Nervo, so we all enjoyed Flannagan and Allen and Nervo and Knox with the Crazy Gang at the Palladium. There was yet another theatre link: another friend, Jock Manby-Colegrave, one of our pre-war ERA drivers, had married a cabaret star called Diana Ward who often came to Brooklands. She had sung at the banquet at the Dorchester in honour of Sir Malcolm Campbell's landspeed record of 301 mph in 1935. Before he bought his ERA, Jock had previously raced MGs. Now he and Diana, forsaking the big Bentleys they had loved, tried an

MG T-type Tickford coupé, which Bill Cotton and I had been driving. They liked it and bought one for themselves, so we all enthused about MGs.

Although Kim and I often talked about MGs, we certainly spent as much time on boats; he was a great sailing man. Yet although for himself he had no time for a craft without sails, he showed great interest and gave me a lot of help with my drawings for a motorcruiser. For both of us, boats were a strong second love. Despite his departure from MG, his heart was still with the cars that he had created. As has been mentioned earlier, he accepted my invitation to join one of our Brains Trusts at a "Rembrandt" meeting. He spoke brilliantly on the design of postwar sports cars, together with George Eyston, Laurence Pomeroy and John Bolster. A few weeks later, Kim and Charles Follett had drinks at my home on Sunday morning and we planned to have dinner, together with George Eyston, the following week. Sad to relate, that dinner did not take place: Kim was tragically killed in an otherwise very minor railway accident at Kings Cross station. There is something especially sad that such a man should die thus. His name and his MG, will be remembered for ever.

As I had hoped, plans for motor racing were occupying more and more of my time as the war was coming to an end. I used to believe that I would start again, more or less where we finished in 1939, with Ray and Peter and the Prideaux-Brunes. However, so much had happened in the war years. The Prideaux-

Party at "Noddings", with the Club Bugatti and Cecil Kimber. The latter is just discernible on the left. This is probably the last photograph of him before his tragic death a few days later.

Brunes had definitely retired from the scene, while Ray and Peter were determined to start an entirely new project to promote a national Grand Prix team. I felt that I would join them in due course, but in the meantime I was happy to help Peter Monkhouse with his aero-engine project at Monaco.

Proud parents.

At Brighton in the 12/60 Alvis: note the lengthened hood to accommodate Peter's carrycot; Penny with Peter and Leonard Potter's Mercedes 540K.

PART III

MOTOR RACING AGAIN

*The first events in England
and Grands Prix
on the Continent*

CHAPTER NINE

In summer 1945, with the war in Europe just over and reasonable petrol ration restored, motor sport was still dormant. I was able, however, to organize an event that proved successful and enjoyable, that at least got racing and sports cars on to a circuit again – albeit a temporary one.

It had been nearly five years since we had had motor racing at Brooklands, Donington, Crystal Palace, Shelsley Walsh and Prescott. At last, some men were being demobilized from the forces, so more dustsheets were being pulled off racing machines.

The recognized motor clubs had been closed down for the duration, so it was taking a long time to get it all started again. Demobilization was a gradual process. As I had been based near London throughout most of the war and able to keep things alive by organizing the "Rembrandt" meetings, everyone expected me to start the ball rolling again with some sort of racing.

We were all getting very restive; no hill or circuit was ready and no club fully reorganized. I went to see Earl Howe, certainly the leading figure in our world of motor racing – as has been mentioned, he was president of the BRDC and also of the ERA Club. He had been an enthusiastic supporter of my "Rembrandt" meetings and, to my great delight, he immediately promised his full backing if I could get anything sensible going again. He said, "Put up a scheme to get racing cars in action again, but not actually racing because of lack of proper tyres and fuel, and I will be with you".

I spent a long time looking for the right venue and eventually found it: a building estate at Cockfosters in Hertfordshire, with a small complex of new roads on an open site, where the houses were not yet started. The owners agreed to hire out the whole estate for one day.

I told Lord Howe about the place and my idea of running racing cars singly and untimed on a tight little circuit, as a demonstration. I drafted the whole proposal and Lord Howe said he would back it, but thought I should put the plan up to the RAC for its approval, which I did. With Lord Howe's approval, the RAC had no objections – but no one there was particularly interested one way or the other. Of course, all the "Rembrandt" organization was behind the scheme and I knew I would have wonderful press backing through Pomeroy and Tubbs in *Motor*, Lindfield in *Autocar*, Findon in *The Light Car* and, of course, more important and most enthusiastically, Bill Boddy in *Motor Sport*. A date was fixed – Saturday 14 July – and our world, our little world, was with me.

There was a great deal of work to be done and some people thought my scheme a terrible gamble. The organization had to start from scratch. We knew we could not provide any proper safety measures, just a line of rope, marshals and the St John Ambulance Brigade. I decided that we would have to restrict the entry to about 30 cars, each driver competing twice. Through the Press we were inundated with requests for entries, so there was the difficult problem of sorting them out and making decisions.

Inevitably, some of the most important entrants had no suitable cars available. The engine of Raymond Mays' ERA R4D was in bits and none of Reg Parnell's many racing cars was in running order, all of them being dismantled. However, some of the best of other cars were available. Bob Gerard had an ERA. Tony Rolt, who had just returned from being a prisoner-of-war in Colditz in Germany, had his ERA R5B all ready for racing – his friend and partner, Jock Horsfall and I had been driving it up and down the road in the hope that we could get something like this organized.

Cockfosters: trying out the course in the Alvis.

Another friend in our locality was George Symonds and we knew his MG R-type was running. John Bolster telephoned me, saying work would go on night and day to have "Bloody Mary" prepared. Of course, we already had the Type 51 Bugatti. I invited Lord Howe to come and drive this as I knew he had nothing in the way of a racing car available. He said he would love to, but felt that something dreadful always happened if you drove anybody else's racing car. He therefore declined the

Eric Findon inspects the course with his Sunbeam-Talbot.

❖ PROGRAMME ❖

THE COCKFOSTERS
RALLY
Thirteenth in a series of meetings arranged for
those interested in the sport of motor racing.
SATURDAY · JULY 14 · 1945
at 2.30 p.m.
Bevan Park Estate
Cockfosters, New Barnet, Herts
IN AID OF THE VICTORIA HOSPITAL, BARNET
Admission 10/- Per Head

The Cockfosters Rally programme.

"Brab" with FLY 1.

invitation to drive our Bugatti, but said that he would come in his own favourite road car, his own Type 57SC coupé, because he felt that his young wife would be more comfortable in that car than in any of the open machines.

As he lived so close, at Finchley, I asked Eric Findon, editor of *The Light Car*, to come and try my course at Cockfosters. He brought his Sunbeam-Talbot, Peter Monkhouse came in the Type 51 Bugatti and I drove my Alvis. We drove round and took photographs, which were published. These boosted publicity for the event.

My friends at Scotland Yard contacted the senior police officer of our area at Cockfosters, who came over and promised every co-operation.

I decided that we would divide the entries between sports and racing cars. We had an excellent selection of mouth-watering sports cars. Flight Lieutenant Anthony Crook, on leave from the RAF, said he would have his 2.9 Alfa Romeo ready, one of the cars raced in the "Fastest Sports Car Race" at Brooklands; "Aldy" (Lieutenant-Colonel H J Aldington), out of uniform, promised that his Frazer Nash-BMW 328 would be ready; the smaller classes were represented by Lieutenant Marcus Chambers on leave from the Royal Navy, with the 1½-litre HRG that he and Peter Clark had been so successful with at Le Mans; and Bob Gerard's very attractive and enthusiastic wife, Joan, was down to drive a Riley Sprite. I kept a few places open before finalizing the lists because of the uncertainty with regard to some entrants. Organizing the officials was quite a problem, because so few of the pre-war people were around. So, as with my wartime "Rembrandts", I gathered together an official organizing committee, which included the MG R-type driver George Symonds and George Bance, the secretary of the recently formed North London Enthusiasts' Car Club, which agreed to provide most of the marshals.

Although the event would not be in any way under the auspices of the RAC, I felt it would be wise to have proper scrutineering. H R Godfrey, of HRG, was therefore appointed official scrutineer. Eric Findon, with his excellent broadcasting and Shelsley Walsh commentating experience, took charge of the public address. Official starters were Eric Giles and Laurence Pomeroy. In fact, "Pom" became a competitor, driving Ariel Clark's 1914 Grand Prix Mercedes, so Eric alone acted as starter for the whole meeting. One of the madly enthusiastic marshals, Kenneth Brown, volunteered to sweep the whole of the circuit early on the morning of the event, to make certain that there were no stones or other rubbish spoiling the look and effectiveness of the track.

About a week before the event, I had a long meeting with Lord Howe and we went through the programme. We were both very conscious of the necessity of preventing any sort of accident, because it would mitigate against the early return to real racing. I therefore wrote a personal letter to every driver, urging restraint, asking them all to put on a show, giving the public the sight, sound and smell of motor racing, but with absolutely no risks at all, since any sort of accident would do the sport a great deal of harm. Last-minute entries I accepted were Lord Brabazon of Tara

MOTOR RACING AGAIN **63**

Opposite Left:
Crowds arriving in the paddock. Bob Gerard's ERA being offloaded from the trailer, with the tea marquee in the background.

Opposite below:
Opening the course with Sybil, Countess Howe, as passenger.

Right:
The "Old Man", complete with carnation in his buttonhole, long cigarette holder and that rakishly angled cap, about to step into his Bugatti 57SC.

Above left:
With Eric Giles and Lord Howe.

Above right:
Lord Brabazon, the Marquess Campden and Lord Howe.

with FLY 1, his lovely little 1100 cc Fiat, and R Gordon Sutherland with a brand-new postwar prototype Aston Martin, the "Atom", which he had already brought to Chessington and some of the "Rembrandts".

Temple Press printed the programme and we decided to charge 10 shillings per head and to give the profits to our local hospital, the Victoria, at Barnet. A great deal of publicity and correspondence indicated the likelihood of a large gate, so we roped in the local squadron of the Air Training Corps to assist the marshals of the NLECC.

Saturday, 14 July 1945 dawned a beautiful sunny day and from 10 am onwards Cockfosters was invaded by motor-racing enthusiasts in or on every sort of car, van, motorcycle, bicycle and on foot. I had the use of a splendid course car, a 1938 4¼-litre Derby Bentley, with Park Ward coachwork and Penny drove her Austin Seven two-seater, checking the marshals' posts and arrangements for the marquee and refreshments. There were many things to be checked, water to be laid on to the tea marquee,

senior officers to be briefed with the police and St John
Ambulance Brigade and a recording unit from the BBC to be
accommodated. At 2.30 pm, with a large public safely behind the
ropes at the "Roundabout", at "Rembrandt Corner", at
"Chessington Bend" and at the "Turn-round", I toured the
circuit in the Bentley with Lord Howe as passenger. He approved
all the arrangements. Then at the wheel of his immaculate Bugatti
57SC with the Countess in the passenger seat, the "Old Man",
complete with long cigarette holder, rakishly angled cap and, of
course, a red carnation in his buttonhole, opened the course with
a good fast run accompanied by considerable applause. At last,
motor racing in Great Britain was off to a splendid new start.

The first entrant, Joan Gerard, immaculate in her white Riley
Sprite, swished round the course, nicely controlled but really
quick, setting a fine example. She smartly reversed at the "Turn-
round" and drove faster at the "Roundabout", while marshals
signalled to Eric Giles that the second car was coming up to his
area. Gordon Sutherland with the "Atom" was another very
popular performer and it was quite an honour to present an
important new car to the public in that way.

Stewart Marshall drove the big ex-Lionel Phillips Leyland
Eight, making a good getaway, but passed out with clutch slip,
so only doing one lap of the semicircle. Both Leslie Ballamy and
"Bunny" Tubbs drove Ballamy's Special. Squadron Leader
Boothby drove his very modern-looking Ford V8-engined Special.

*John James in the ex-
Malcolm Campbell
Mercedes SSK now owned
by Ronald Stern.*

George Symmonds opens the racing class with the MG R-type.

Charles Brackenbury said to me, "I suppose you know what you are doing, Rivers, letting all these new boys drive racing cars." He and Freddie Dixon reckoned that 90 per cent of the people in the paddock had never seen motor racing in their lives. I think they were wrong, but nearly five years is a long time and a generation of young schoolboys had grown to maturity in record time. In any case, it was inevitable that old hands felt some resentment about newcomers appearing on the scene.

V S Biggs drove a four-seater Allard. T G Tice appeared with the very special streamlined V12 Lagonda that had been driven at Brooklands just before the war, at a time when the streamlined Bentley saloon made a record attempt.

Louis Giron drove a Bugatti Type 55. Needless to say, someone reported him as "Louis Chiron", although I had warned Eric Findon to make a clear distinction, which I know he did. Even so, quite a lot of people thought they were watching the famous French ace Grand Prix driver.

Another "Fastest Sports Car" entrant was Dorothy Patten, Baroness d'Orndorff, at the wheel of the Peugeot her husband, "Danny" d'Orndorff, drove at Brooklands. One of the neatest and fastest sports cars was Gordon Claridge's BMW 328.

Mann drove an SS 100, which was a good choice, although at that time we never envisaged the future Jaguar successes at Le Mans. The ex-Malcolm Campbell Mercedes 38/250 that John James brought to the event formed a confusing footnote: although never a works car it was white; Campbell had always had it painted blue.

Before the racing class performed we had an interval with teas served in the marquee overlooking the paddock, while most of the spectators examined the cars and met the drivers. George Symonds opened the racing class with his MG R-type, effectively demonstrating the unusual stance of that car. Bob Gerard put on

At the "Turnround": T C Tice in the streamlined Lagonda V12, later restored by Brian Morgan.

Dorothy Patten, Baroness d'Orndorff, in her Peugeot.

Above:
Bob Gerard's ERA foreshadowing great achievements with that car.

Right:
Charles Mortimer's Alfa Romeo.

Below:
Laurence Pomeroy peering through his monocle driving Ariel Clark's 1914 Mercedes; the owner is in the passenger seat.

the first ERA performance, making us all feel we were really back to pre-war racing as his car's exhaust note thrilled the spectators. Another favourite car of mine was the 2.6-litre Monza Alfa Romeo, driven by Charles Mortimer. The vintage scene was represented by Anthony Heal with his 1919 5-litre Ballot, by "Pom" driving Ariel Clark's 1914 Grand Prix Mercedes and by the sensational John Bolster with his "Bloody Mary". John was the only person to spin his car round instead of reversing at the "Turn-round".

Although there were no official times, a number of people unofficially timed each performance. John Bolster's demonstration proved to be the unofficial fastest time of the day. Peter Monkhouse made a very fast run in the Bugatti Club's Type 51, leaving long black lines on the concrete at the start. Perhaps the most popular performance of all was the famous ex-B. Bira ERA R5B "Remus" driven by Tony Rolt and his partner, Jock Horsfall.

Everything went without a hitch, amid tremendous enthusiasm and in perfect weather. People took their time packing up the cars as they renewed pre-war motor racing friendships. Then as soon as everything was cleared up, the heavens opened and we had a torrential downpour.

That night, the BBC radio news carried a good account of the event. It was also adequately covered by the national press, while our own motoring journals reported almost every detail with great enthusiasm. A substantial cheque was presented to the Victoria Hospital at Barnet as the profits from the Cockfosters Rally. In this way British motor sport started again after the end of the Second World War.

Tony Rolt, not long back from Colditz, drew the biggest round of applause at the wheel of the ERA R5B "Remus".

Above:
Peter Monkhouse with the Bugatti Owners' Club car.

Above left:
The irrepressible John Bolster's "Bloody Mary".

Above right:
John Dowson in the Lightweight Special.

Right:
Eric Giles with the starter's flag and Anthony Heal in the Ballot.

CHAPTER TEN

Hugh Green, whom we knew as a Type 50 Bugatti owner and Monaco customer, approached us about buying an ERA. He had some motorcycle club racing experience, but now wanted to move into the fastest category of car racing. He said that, if we could find the right ERA car and would prepare it for him, he would like to share the driving with me, because of my previous experience with the ERA company. This suited me well, as I knew that Tony Rolt was on to a new project and keen to sell the R5B "Remus" he had been sharing with Jock Horsfall. Jock had already asked if we could find a customer and I knew the car was in splendid condition. Jock and I demonstrated the ERA up and down the Watford bypass. Hugh Green agreed to buy and we drew up an agreement. I would have the first drive and an announcement was made through the press.

The Bristol Aeroplane Company Motor Sports Club announced a more or less private sprint on the firm's own airfield at Filton. This was to be a very low-key affair, with no public and only a few non-members invited to compete. The event was for bikes and cars, as there was a predominance of motorcycle-owning members in the promoting club. Invitations to compete came to Monaco Motors and to Jock Horsfall. We entered the ERA for me to drive. Hugh Green entered a Rudge and Jock Horsfall an

Monaco advertisement.

HRD bike. A telephone call from Bob Gerard told me that he was entering   ERA. I went to Leicester to look at the car, which was an R2A, Pat Fairfield's original 1100 cc, but now with a 1½-litre engine and crash gearbox instead of the preselector. The only previous ERA so fitted had been   R9B, which Denis Scribbans tried with a Riley crash box. I remembered the car very well, because he had won his very first event in it at Brooklands, but with the normal preselector gearbox.

I was getting very excited about my drive in the ERA and Jock and I had another test run. However, there was a snag: Hugh Green was obviously having some difficulty in getting together the remaining money to complete the purchase. So, a week before the event, we had to scratch the ERA and I had to run my 12/60 Alvis instead.

It was a strange feeling to be going to a motoring event that I was not responsible for after five years of being in charge. For a moment I think I resented it: the sport of motor racing had been mine for so long. Now, I had to hand over the reins. I had been a privileged caretaker and now, suddenly, the world was coming

Above left:
Hugh Green on his Rudge with Charlie Lucas.

Above right:
Jock Horsfall demonstrating the ERA to Hugh Green on the offside of the car.

right again; our sport was back where it belonged and motor clubs were running the events.

Sunday, 28 October 1945, was terribly wet; it rained all day, making the Filton sprint a rather damp squib. Bob Gerard ran away with the FTD; John Bolster in "Bloody Mary" and Dowson in the Lightweight Special both had good runs, despite a lot of wheelspin on the wet tarmac. Dennis Poore ran a supercharged 747 cc MG and Sydney Allard was very quick in a new Allard. In our équipe, we had some success because Jock Horsfall was the fastest bike. Hugh Green had a good ride and I quite enjoyed my run in the Alvis – although sprints on a straight course are not very thrilling unless you are driving something fairly fast.

The 750 Club ran a gymkhana event and we all had a lot of fun on a damp grass course. I drove the Alvis. One of the marshals was Denis Jenkinson. The Vintage Sports Car Club kicked off with a very good Marlowe trial. Penny acted as my navigator in the Alvis and coped very well with a timed plug change, which was part of the competition. The Alvis seemed quite good at that sort of trial and we were furthest up the hill among the pre-war cars on one of the slippery slopes. By that time, I was a committee member of the VSCC and was enjoying all the committee meetings under the president, Forrest Lycett, in whose London flat we always met.

The Hugh Green ERA project, which had such good prospects for me, failed very sadly. Hugh Green never completed the purchase, so I decided that I would have to buy something for my own racing. With a baby son to consider and practically no capital at all, I had to look for something very moderate to replace the Alvis for general transport, as well as any racing that could come my way.

A visit to Bourne to see Raymond Mays and Peter Berthon, found them obviously much more interested in their new national Grand Prix car project than in getting the R4D ready for racing. Ray had tried hard to convince the principal British car manufacturers to back his project, with no success at all. Now he told me that his approach to the Society of Motor Manufacturers and Traders had met a negative response, so he was compiling a letter to all the leading accessory and supporting companies in the motor industry. Peter Berthon had a young draughtsman working with him outlining a new car, a very advanced V16 supercharged 1½-litre to challenge the postwar Italian cars that were dominating the international Grand Prix scene. I remembered that Peter had really wanted a V8 ERA engine for the E-type before the war, but there was never any chance of getting that amount of money for a completely new power unit.

The new project was going to be called the BRM (British Racing Motors), which had been the alternative name suggested in 1934 for the ERA (English Racing Automobiles). At that time, Humphrey Cook believed that the ERA would probably be called the "Era", just as the Italian FIAT was referred to as the "Fiat". BRM had in fact been proposed first, because these initials also suggested Berthon – Raymond – Mays.

Peter's first sketches of the BRM looked very like the E-type ERA, with the same independent front suspension. It was very exciting, but they were talking about many thousands of pounds, a level of expenditure way above what we were used to in Britain.

I asked about a job for me in the project and was told that I would be with them in due course, when they had a full Grand Prix team. I realized that that would be in the fairly distant future. In the meantime, my own first priority was to get racing going on the right lines in this country, no longer on my own now that the clubs were getting their act together. Many of them had been used to my arranging events and so I was often brought into meetings and negotiations for new circuits. Committee meetings of the VSCC, under the presidency of Forrest Lycett, were always interesting as the club was very much in the foreground in promoting the sport.

Although not a member of the Junior Car Club, I attended several of its meetings with Charles Follett. The leading light was "Bunny" Dyer, who certainly had been the best and most forward-thinking race organizer in Great Britain before the war.

It was obvious that Brooklands was finished as a racing circuit for much of the banking had been demolished and there were factories and other buildings growing out of what used to be the rest of the track. Everything was against the future of the track for racing, including the fact that nothing could have been done about the unbanked and partly blind corner on the outer circuit at the fork. Lap speeds of over 150 mph could never have been envisaged in 1906-7 when H F Locke King built Brooklands.

The pre-war Mercedes and Auto Unions did not race at Brooklands and would never have done so. Looking towards the 1950s, it was obvious that we should be considering a new track,

VSCC Marlowe trial with the Alvis: Penny changes a plug while the author changes a wheel; David Render operates the clock – not FTD, but not bad.

possibly combining the steep banking of the German Avus with a genuine road circuit like the Nürburgring.

When the demolished track was sold, the JCC very sensibly bought the assets of the old Brooklands Automobile Racing Club. The JCC was renamed the British Automobile Racing Club, thus retaining the traditional initials. I suggested a fund to build a new national circuit, but was told that such things would have to wait a while.

There was a good deal of pressure to carry on with "Rembrandt" meetings after the war and I considered starting a permanent motor club in London. The Rembrandt Hotel was a natural venue and its management was prepared to consider the project. I found I could get the required financial backing, but I could not see myself running the club – it was just not my sort of occupation.

While I was wondering who could join me, Johnnie Morgan of the JCC and Desmond Scannell of the BRDC opened the Steering Wheel Club in Brick Street. It was a great success right from the start. I was delighted to be a founder member and for many years "the Wheel" was the hub and centre of motor sport in Great Britain. The little premises just off Park Lane were ideal for what was the small world of motor racing at that time and, quite appropriately, it was the office of the BRDC.

Peter Monkhouse and I took the Duke-Woolley MG, originally produced for the 1939 TT, to John Thornley at Abingdon. He tried it and was very impressed. We told him that we wanted to market the racing TT model ourselves in small batches, so please could we have the first six TC chassis? He told us it was impossible; we could not have even one. Almost the entire production of TCs, the first postwar MG (1946), was going to America for much-needed dollars. He would only let the top MG distributors in this country have an occasional one. So, unfortunately, our Monaco TT racing MG project was a non-starter.

Peter and I became involved in the design and development of an overhead valve conversion for the Ford V8 engine with a charming and brilliant American designer, Zora Arkus-Duntov from Detroit. We had a lot of fun with Allards and plans for an entirely new American sports car. We went to the Speedway at Wembley several times because Zora was also interested in Midget racing cars.

I took him out in the Duke-Woolley MG. He thought it was most amusing, but could not believe that it would be accepted as a real sports car in America. He was proved quite wrong about that – and of course we learned later that his new American car turned out to be the Chevrolet Corvette, which first appeared in 1953.

CHAPTER ELEVEN

In the meantime I was extremely worried about the future of motor sport. Lord Howe had said that he would back me in any good scheme to get racing going, but where? There was no track available. I contacted all the circuit owners: Brooklands was built over and obviously impossible; I knew that Donington was also partly built over and was in permanent use by a government ministry and this was confirmed in writing; I knew that Crystal Palace was not possible at all. I even tried two of the old motorcycle circuits, but they were not available either.

There was, however an obvious easy solution: the many splendid wartime airfields with fine runways, large areas of tarmac and big hangars. It was quite obvious that most of these airfields were now "surplus to requirements" and some were completely deserted with empty hangars. I contacted the RAC which, even with the backing of Lord Howe, merely said that no airfields were available. In those days the RAC, although the senior club, was not responsible for all motor sport as it is now. It was not by any means the most active motor club in respect of racing. I reckoned that the BRDC and the JCC had been the most active before the war and were the best bet to get racing going again, so I lobbied them continuously, but without any success at all. Leading members of the Vintage Sports Car Club and the Bugatti Owners' Club had been very helpful with regard to my "Rembrandt" meetings and Cockfosters. I therefore suggested that we should make a joint approach to the Air Ministry for the use of any available airfield for a VSCC/BOC sprint. This request was turned down. Then senior members of the BRDC, JCC and VSCC wrote further letters, telephoned and made personal visits to the Air Ministry, who alone could permit the use of the airfields.

It seemed that neither the chairman of the RAC nor Lord Howe, or anyone at the top of motor racing in this country, could obtain the permission we needed from the Air Ministry. My own personal visits carried no weight at all, because I was just someone who had been doing things on his own and was in no way officially representing our world of motor racing.

Lord Brabazon had been most helpful in other directions, had come to the "Rembrandts" and had driven his Fiat, FLY 1, at Cockfosters. Although he was no longer the Minister of Aircraft Production, I suggested that I should go and see him on behalf of the VSCC with regard to the use of airfields for racing. This was agreed. When I told him how emphatically the Air Ministry had refused, he said that it was outrageous and that of course we should be able to use those empty wartime airfields for motor racing now. He said, "I am sure we can get permission, if we contact the right man".

Lord Brabazon told me that the most influential man in the Ministry was young Peter Masefield, who had been so helpful to us with our aero-engine. Although it was not his department at all, "Brab" was convinced that Masefield, who in any case was very keen on motor racing and was a close friend of Whitney Straight, had more influence at the Ministry than anyone else when it came to getting special things done. He said that we should go and see Masefield together. However, I had first to decide exactly what I wanted and when. A complete proposition had to be prepared with all details.

I reported back to Forrest Lycett, president of the VSCC, Tim Carson, the club secretary and two members of the committee who had already visited Elstree airfield and had got the backing of the officer in charge there. We drafted a plan for a two-at-a-time sprint, with three or four suggested dates. "Brab" and I took this to Peter Masefield. He was very enthusiastic and within a few days I had a telephone call from "Brab" to say that the Air Ministry had given permission for the event. The date was fixed: Easter Bank Holiday, April 1946.

At last, we had cracked it! Lord Howe invited "Brab" and me to lunch at the RAC to celebrate the achievement and I reckoned there would be no stopping us now. I was in favour of telling the RAC and all the other clubs who they should contact and apply to for possible dates and airfields. "Brab", however, cautioned me, saying that we must make certain that Elstree was a great success, with no accidents, before going any further. This was to be the first big motor event since the war: Cockfosters had been the curtain raiser; Filton had been very low key, at a private venue and not open to the public; but Elstree was going to be the real thing! We felt we would get a good and important entry, with many spectators.

I very much hoped that Raymond Mays would bring out his ERA R4D, but he was still waiting for some parts to be machined. I thought it would have been very appropriate for Ray to achieve fastest time of the day in that car, in the first real motor racing event after the war. Peter Monkhouse telephoned Hamish Weir, telling him that his Magnette would be ready for Elstree, but only just. It would be unpainted: would he race it? Weir said he could not arrange to come to England at that time. Would Rivers Fletcher, who had done most of the testing, drive for him? The author did not need any persuading! As well as the Weir Magnette, Hector Graham from Ireland brought his ex-JHT Smith K3 for us to prepare for the event. Peter himself was going to drive the Type 51 Bugatti and Leslie Johnson entered

Opposite right:
Testing the Monaco MG K3 on the Watford bypass, with trade plates and *very* **detachable wings.**

the Darracq. I also entered my 12/60 Alvis, so we were more than heavily involved.

The fortnight before Easter was very hectic, but incredibly enjoyable, as we were testing racing cars every day and I had to do a lot of running in with the Weir K3. We fitted light detachable wings, which sometimes flew off: the driver, without any protective windscreen, had to take care not to be decapitated! At first we used a straight-through exhaust pipe, but it was so noisy that we found the old Brooklands expansion chamber that Peter had used on his racing P-type and fitted that. We also tried to remember the trade plates! Leslie Johnson was too busy in his big furniture business to do any of the testing on the Darracq: as I knew the car quite well, he asked me to take his place in the event, if he was allowed to drive his own BMW 328 instead. This was arranged and it was decided that Peter and I would share the driving in the Darracq.

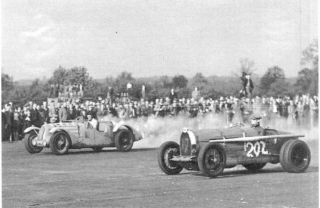

On Good Friday and Easter Saturday, Peter and I did final testing on all the cars on the Watford bypass; all was set for the big meeting on Easter Monday. The weather was perfect and an enormous crowd descended upon the Elstree airfield, many more than we had ever expected – in fact, about 20,000 people attended. It was one of the best days in my life! We lined up our team of cars in the paddock, giving us a big circle for testing and warming up, but there was only a single line of rope to hold back the public from the course, which was a mere 400 ft of the main runway and slightly uphill with a very good run-off at the end. We had a splendid entry of nearly 100 cars and about 30 bikes, so the regulations stipulated one run for everyone and second runs only if time permitted. The surface of the course was rather peculiar, being a mixture of tar and wood chips.

Even in the dry it was exceedingly slippery so, had it been wet, there would have been phenomenal wheelspin all the way. There was some delay at the start because the electrical timing apparatus was playing up, so hand timing was used; but it seemed quite satisfactory. Crowd control, which was the job of the NLECC, was excellently done, despite that rudimentary single line of rope.

Although Raymond Mays and his R4D were sadly missed, there was a first-class racing entry, which included Reg Parnell's 1½-litre Delage to be driven by his cousin, Roy Parnell, his 4CLT

Left:
Elstree with the Monaco cars lined up in the paddock: the Monaco MG K3; Hector Graham's K3; Leslie Johnson's Darracq; the Club Bugatti; and our works Wolseley Fourteen.

Right:
Kenneth Bear with twin rear wheels beats the author off the line, where the tyre smoke shows he is using too much wheelspin.

Maserati to be driven by Reg himself and his Dixon-Riley; George Abecassis' Alta; Bob Gerard's ERA; Bob Cowell driving the new (ex-Lady Mary Grosvenor) 2-litre Alta; Charles Mortimer's Alta; David Hampshire's Maserati 6C; John Bolster with his "Bloody Mary"; together with Peter Monkhouse with the Bugatti Type 51.

With Gordon Wilkins, Leslie Johnson and Tommy Doman, and Leslie's Frazer Nash-BMW 328.

There was also another ERA, R1A driven by a newcomer, J B Heath and more Bugattis, including Kenneth Bear's big 4.9, which ran as a sports car against our Darracq. Our two K3s, to be driven by Hector Graham and me, were much the fastest

With Peter Monkhouse and "Beano" Ibbotson, with Jaguar and Alfa Romeo. This Jaguar was a 3½-litre saloon kept as an extra Works hack. There was a lot of mileage on the clock, but it was fast and reliable.

MGs. There was a fine selection of Bentleys, Vauxhalls, Frazer Nashes and Rileys among the sports cars; together with much older machines, such as Sumner's Isotta-Fraschini, two Grand Prix Sunbeams, Anthony Heal's Fiat, John Bolster's Rolls-Royce Silver Ghost and Bill Boddy with a Hispano-Suiza Alfonso. That is only a selection of the enormous entry, plus the 30 bikes.

My 12/60 Alvis performed quite well, just beating Clarke's identical TK 12/60 off the line, but dead heating at the final. Then I came to the line with the Weir MG alongside Hector Graham, as we were paired for the 1100 cc racing class. In my ERA days, before the war, I had learned from Raymond Mays a cunning way of making a racing getaway, valuable on a slippery start when you needed both hands at the wheel, keeping the car straight for a considerable distance. I reckoned this would be invaluable at Elstree. On the line, I engaged first gear and let in the clutch (technically the gear-changing pedal) until it just started to bite. Then I engaged second gear on the quadrant, but did not depress the clutch. This enabled me to keep both hands on the wheel, keeping the car straight right through to maximum revs on first, just dabbing the clutch to engage second while still steering with both hands until I needed to engage third gear. It worked like a charm: my car kept straight while Hector Graham lost a lot of time getting his machine sideways when he engaged second; so we won our class.

Peter Monkhouse, who made a splendid FTD, pushing the gear lever into second.

Now, we had the very fast machines. Roy Parnell, very much a newcomer, made a splendid run in the Delage, faster than Reg in the Maserati. Then Peter Monkhouse made an absolutely splendid start with the Club Bugatti, achieving fastest time of the day in 15.2 seconds against Roy Parnell with 15.8. My time with the Magnette was 18.6 seconds. Peter, in the Darracq, was faster than me because I had too much wheelspin and Leslie Johnson won his class with the BMW.

Despite the large entry, we all had second runs. Few of us,

however, made better times, because the course had become much more slippery. In fact, several people spun, including Hector Graham; but the day was a fabulous success, particularly for us at Monaco Motors.

The way ahead was clear: the clubs could count on support from competitors and the public. Eric Giles, for the Bugatti Owners' Club and Leslie Wilson for the MAC, announced that Prescott and Shelsley Walsh would be ready for racing as soon as possible. The JCC people said they would be looking into likely airfields for early resumption of racing: even the RAC put "Airfields for motor racing" on the agenda for its next committee meeting.

My job, keeping Monaco Engines full of machining jobs and arranging the workload, was being much helped by having a young and pretty private secretary. Esme Temple had good previous experience with Kodak at Harrow. She soon became involved with the paperwork of motor racing, which led to her joining us at racing events. Since Penny and I were nearly always joined by my lifelong friend "Beano" Ibbotson, we formed a very happy foursome.

Easter 1946 was a wonderful time, Easter Monday one of the best days of my life. Taking stock of my life to date, I reckoned that I had been very lucky indeed. My dream, my daydream, was all coming true. Of course, I had a flying start, riding with Malcolm Campbell in 1928, when I was only sixteen. Then I was spoiled by Woolf Barnato at Bentley when I served my apprenticeship with that company and he let me drive some of his great cars. I had a close relationship with Earl Howe and Whitney Straight and their racing; then Raymond Mays and Peter Berthon with the Villiers Supercharge, Invicta, Riley and ERAs. My founding the ERA Club led to my joining Mays and Berthon. Although the Second World War had stopped everything, again it was ridiculously lucky for me: a perilous life at sea with the Royal Naval Reserve never took place and my jobs in the London area with people I already knew in motor racing enabled me to keep the sport going. Now, through Lord Brabazon and Peter Masefield, we were racing again at last. Moreover, I was racing myself and even winning my class in what must have been the fastest 1100 cc racing car of those times.

I thought the world was my oyster. It was not, of course. In truth, I had just been very, very lucky. My job as the commercial manager and production controller of Monaco Engines Limited was happy enough in itself because my boss, Peter Monkhouse, was also a great friend. We also both spent a large proportion – probably too large a proportion – of our time on motor racing with the other company at Watford, where John Wyer and Ian Nichols had joined Ian Connell.

Although the business I did with AEC Limited at Southall and our other contractors showed a reasonable profit, it never made enough to cover the escalating cost of developing the new aero-engine. The situation at Monaco Engines was therefore somewhat precarious.

Now I decided it was high time I had a real competition car for myself, but it had to be my everyday transport as well. Penny had her own Austin Seven, but we could not afford three cars. Thus the Alvis had to be replaced with something more nimble. I knew exactly what I wanted, something that I had in mind before the outbreak of the war: an 1100 cc Singer-engined HRG. The works car I had tried in the autumn of 1939 was one that I really liked. I reckoned that I would try to find one and, if I failed, I would go for a Morgan or an MG P-type. I was lucky, for within a few weeks Guy Robbins of HRG rang to say that he had a splendid little 1939 1100 cc model, the only one that used the big external petrol tank as fitted to the 1½-litre. I dashed over to Tolworth and tried it. It was in splendid condition, with a very small mileage and it was blue. "HPJ 399" was mine. I soon found a keen buyer for my Alvis, which had been an excellent proposition, requiring no attention at all, but was not quite fast enough for the sprints, hillclimbs and races I had in mind.

Below left:
The HRG.

Below right:
Peter Monkhouse's Alfa Romeo drophead coupé.

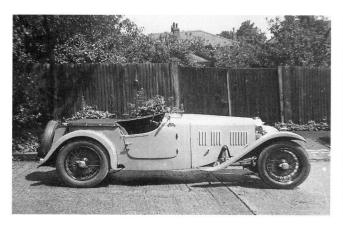

At the Monaco works Peter Monkhouse did a little tuning of the engine of the HRG and I had the car resprayed in my own paler blue. The space behind the front seats was just right for Peter's carrycot and both Penny and I enjoyed every mile at the wheel of the little "Hurg".

Peter Monkhouse bought a fine 2.3 Alfa Romeo drophead coupé for his general use and we often shared the driving on journeys to Vickers at Brooklands, airfields in East Anglia, Oxford and the Midlands. Peter was an exceptionally good fast driver on the road, but impatient and intolerant of other slower traffic, which was his character anyway. Nevertheless, he gave great confidence because of his superb judgment. I enjoyed being his passenger, even when he was having a great go, cornering near the limit on the open road. When I drove him he seemed quite happy, although I never went anywhere near as fast as he did. Other well-known motor racing personalities with whom I felt completely happy and relaxed, however fast they drove, included Malcolm Campbell, Woolf Barnato, Raymond Mays, Sammy Davis and George Eyston. Others with whom I was much less relaxed included Earl Howe, Peter Berthon and the technical editor of *Motor*, Laurence Pomeroy.

PART IV

NEW PROJECTS

*Our own racing with HRG and MG.
New projects for ERA and a
National Grand Prix car*

CHAPTER TWELVE

Nearly all the motor clubs were coming to life again. Stringent petrol rationing still prevented the really large-scale events, but there were ever-increasing numbers of small local meetings, rallies and trials. We ran the HRG in every possible event, saw quite a lot of the works and the firm's directors and enjoyed the set-up.

The charm of the HRG was its vintage style, so the company's streamlined version had no appeal, although I enjoyed a drive in one. Penny and I took our baby son Peter – with all the resultant luggage – to Salcombe in Devon, where we were joined by the artist Roy Nockolds. Roy and I dashed up and down the Devon hills in the little "Hurg". Roy sketched me sailing, but said he much preferred illustrating cars and aircraft.

Having started the ball rolling by getting Air Ministry permission for racing on a wartime airfield, I thought it would subsequently be plain sailing for lots of circuit racing straight away. Several applications were made, but they all took a long time to negotiate. One of the smaller groups, the Cambridge University Automobile Club, was very quick off the mark. The club officials were friends of the Vintage Sports Car Club and we were able to help. The CUAC was the first club to get a permit, but it was by no means easy and a good deal of high level discussion took place before the date was fixed: Saturday, 15 June 1946.

Peter Monkhouse and I entered the Bugatti Type 51 and my HRG and we also prepared cars for several customers as well. Hamish Weir entered the Monaco K3, now painted black and we had other MGs, Alfa Romeos and BMWs to prepare and test. The meeting was held at Gransden Lodge, near Cambridge, a very large and of course absolutely flat mass of concrete runways. Everything looked promising except the weather; it rained heavily all through practice in the morning and racing in the afternoon.

The paddock was inside a very large hangar, which certainly kept us dry, but the noise was appalling. After being used to tracks like Brooklands, Donington and Crystal Palace, the circuit at Gransden Lodge was a very new thing and different from anything we had experienced. It was a simple triangle, with pylons marking the three corners and many flags and straw bales. Practice time was spent finding our way. There was an ocean of space everywhere, but where exactly to go? The fact that it was raining all the time did not help.

I was in the first race, a three-lap scratch event for 1100 cc sports cars. I enjoyed it, but found it impossible to decide on a good line at the corners. I was beaten to third place by Joe Lowrey in an identical HRG, who cornered better than I did. The fastest in our race was Doug Wilcox in a very hot supercharged MG Midget, but he lost it by spinning several times and the Brooklands driver, Le Strange Metcalf, won quite easily in his Fiat Balilla.

Penny with the HRG at Brighton. My cousin Richard and his wife are behind the HRG with their very attractive and rare 1938 Austin Seven two-seater.

There were 11 more short scratch races and plenty of spins! Nearly all the Elstree competitors ran and quite a lot of newcomers as well. Alec Issigonis won his race in the beautiful Lightweight Special and Joan Gerard was very neat and fast in the Riley Sprite, finishing second to Peter Clark's HRG. The MG Magnettes we prepared did very well with Ian Nickols just pipping Hamish Weir in the car I had driven at Elstree.

Reg Parnell's Maserati and George Abecassis' Alta were the fastest 1½-litres, beating Bob Gerard and Bainbridge in their ERAs, who both had spins. Peter Monkhouse had a good day

Above:
First meeting with Ronnie Mountford at Prescott.

Left:
HRG and Bugatti at the Monaco Works.

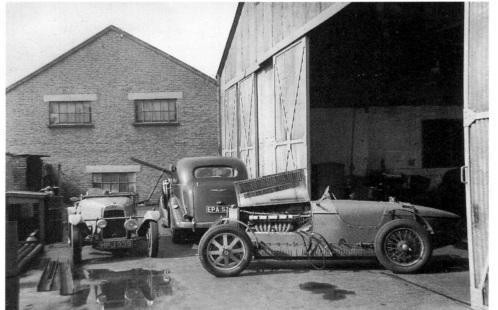

with the Bugatti Type 51, finishing second in his first race and very nearly taking another second place in the final event, but he lost his way at the pylons on the last corner. The fastest car of all was Abecassis' 3.3 Bugatti. In the final race he, too, had a spin in the appalling conditions. It was very unfortunate that we had such terrible weather for the first circuit race since the war. However, despite the weather and the difficulties on a new circuit with problems, the young club was well up to the organization and there were no serious incidents to mar the important occasion.

Tommy Doman driving Leslie Johnson's Frazer Nash-BMW at Prescott.

After the successes at Elstree and Gransden Lodge, we had a couple of disappointing meetings. A friend entered me as his driver in his very special Aston Martin for the May event at Prescott. The car was potentially very interesting: a 1932 International fitted with a 30 hp Ford V8 engine with an overhead valve head conversion. However, it was not quite ready, for only one bank of cylinders had the overhead valve conversion while the other still retained the standard side valves. The scrutineers were not very happy with quite a lot of things. I had a cautious practice run and thought the car did not steer at all! The RAC steward, Sammy Davis, advised me to withdraw. However, the owner himself asked permission to drive instead and he was allowed to practise. On his first run he spun at Orchard. He then reversed back to the start, which was contrary to regulations. He lost control at the start line and collided with the club steward's Bugatti. Needless to say, the car was posted a non-starter.

For Shelsley Walsh, Dorothy Patten, the Baroness d'Orndorff, entered me to drive her very fast Peugeot. Dorothy was a very good "press on" driver herself and I had already shared a drive with her in her Speed 220 Alvis. She was however, a newcomer to Shelsley and that was why I was entered as her driver. At the last moment, Dorothy telephoned to say that the car was not ready, so again I was a non-starter. Penny came with me to

Shelsley in the HRG supporting Raymond Mays with his ERA. It was a wet Shelsley, just as it had been on my first visit there in 1930 when Ray was driving the Villiers Supercharge. However, despite the weather, it was a very good meeting and Ray made a good FTD, just beating Ken Hutchison, who was driving the ex-Ashby Dubonnet front-suspended monoposto Alfa Romeo. I was particularly interested to see "B. Bira" driving the ex-Whitney Straight 2.9-litre Maserati. He was typically neat and tidy, but I thought he was not really sufficiently aggressive. Speed hillclimbing requires a special technique of going absolutely flat out right from the start – something quite different from the prince's very successful racetrack skills.

For the July Prescott hillclimb we competed with the HRG. I had driven there from home in the "Hurg" and, after my first practice run, we were standing by the car in the paddock. I noticed a young man who was taking a special interest in the car, so I spoke to him. I learned that his name was Ronnie Mountford and he was quite familiar with the car, having known

Brighton speed trials: "B Bira" in the Maserati with Ray, Bob Cowell and the author.

its previous owner. Ronnie Mountford proved to be a fount of knowledge. As he was on his own, he joined us for the rest of the practice. When I changed down to first gear for Orchard corner on my last run of the afternoon, the gear lever broke at the bottom, leaving me no alternative but to continue slowly up the hill in first gear. Back in the paddock, we started to remove the gear change mechanism. Ronnie soon saw that I was fairly hopeless as a mechanic, so he took charge of the situation. There was not enough "meat" at the bottom of the gear lever to fit a sleeve, so the only repair possible was welding. No one had any welding equipment at Prescott and it was too late to get it done at nearby Cheltenham or Tewkesbury. We knew that the only likely spare would be from a Le Mans Singer Nine: the 1100 cc HRG was using that model of engine and gearbox. Ronnie said he would go to the entrance of Prescott early on Sunday morning and tackle the owner of the first Le Mans Singer to arrive.

Quite early on Sunday, well before the start of the meeting, a Le Mans Singer Nine coupé came through the entrance gate in the public enclosure. The single occupant was a man who had never been to a motor racing event before. Imagine his surprise when Ronnie opened the passenger door and climbed in saying, "Please excuse me; do you mind if I remove your gear lever as one of the competitors needs it? I will refit it immediately after the racing". While Ronnie was talking, he was unscrewing the remote control mechanism of the gearbox. The poor driver was completely bewildered and asked if this sort of thing was usual. By the time he had grasped the situation, Ronnie had removed his gear lever and locked his gearbox into first gear so that he was able to park the car. Ronnie gave him a paddock pass and a programme, marking my HRG so that he could follow the progress of his gear lever. He also invited him to visit us for a drink in the paddock after the meeting, while he refitted the gear lever. The whole thing worked like a charm – we had two good runs and Ronnie fitted the gear lever when it was all over. The Singer driver was very decent about it; I wonder if this put him off the sport, or did it make his day?

After this first encounter, Ronnie joined us for all the meetings for the rest of the season. He had served his engineering apprenticeship at Austin at the time of the lovely little twin-cam, single-seater works cars, when the conductors were Driscoll, Hadley and Goodacre. Ronnie proved to be a devoted disciple of Sammy Davis, sports editor of the *Autocar*, who was of course an old friend of mine by that time. The rest of our season with the HRG was most enjoyable. We ran in another Prescott, the Vintage event, in the Brighton speed trials, a couple of rallies and the West Court speed trials at Finchampstead organized by the Hants and Berks Motor Club. There we were second in our class, getting a rather nice silver eggcup.

We wanted real racing. If only we still had the Brooklands track we could have had racing straight away. Bill Boddy was determined to see if the old circuit could be rebuilt, forming the Brooklands Society to that end. Lord Montagu took the chair at the inaugural meeting and there was great enthusiasm for saving at least the best part of Brooklands. Bill Boddy and I served on the first committee and we all tried to rescue the old place. It seemed rather a long shot, but Kenneth Evans and Vaughan Davis managed to prevent the destruction of a lot of the track, although actual racing still seemed unlikely.

While we were getting excited about some sprints, there was real circuit racing on the Continent. Louis Chiron drove his $4\frac{1}{2}$-litre unblown Talbot from his native Monte Carlo to Nice for the Grand Prix, which was the first real postwar motor race in France. He was joined by Raymond Sommer, with an Alfa Romeo and Luigi Villoresi with a $1\frac{1}{2}$-litre Maserati. At Nice, it was a simple street race, just like the one they ran before the war, with most of the circuit up and down the Promenade des Anglais, by the Hotel Negresco. Villoresi won quite easily. We heard all about this from John Eason-Gibson, one of the few Britons present. It seemed strangely unfair: we had won the war, but quite a lot of our former enemies were back in racing before us. I lobbied the RAC and had a long meeting with Earl Howe and Raymond Mays. It seemed that the main obstacle was the same old pre-war snag: the law of the land preventing any motor racing on public roads in Britain. On top of that I thought that our administration was a bit lethargic. The "Old Man" said he would call a meeting in London of all the clubs to try and get something done.

It all sounded quite promising. However, as we were parting after the lunch, Howe called me back and said, "It will be an uphill fight, so go on fighting yourself; but I will back you with the BRDC behind us". That gave me heart. At that time I did think that we would soon be back racing everywhere with a fine British team of our own, led by Raymond Mays; rather like our old ERA project, but this time for full-scale Grand Prix events instead of at voiturette level.

There was more Continental racing at Marseilles and even in Paris itself, where T.A.S.O. Mathieson drove a 2½-litre Maserati against Tazio Nuvolari and Jean-Pierre Wimille. We heard that "Taso" had been well up among the fastest until the car broke down.

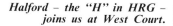

Halford – the "H" in HRG – joins us at West Court.

An entirely new development was a garage business called Raymond Mays & Partners, opposite the old ERA works. The Prideaux-Brunes had closed their Winter Garden Garages in London and sold the premises. They now financed Ray in the new business at Bourne. Typically, the Prideaux-Brunes did not want their name to be publicized with the project. Lancelot and Charlotte were very self-effacing and modest people, supporting Ray again just as they had done with the Raymond Mays Special cars and the ERA R4D before the war. The new company was run by Henry Coy, another good friend who had been with ERA. The fine new premises with showrooms and workshops specialized in Rolls-Royce, Bentley, Rover and Standard cars, which also emphasized Ray's continued loyalty to those makes.

On the line with the HRG at West Court.

CHAPTER THIRTEEN

The first postwar event on the Continent of Europe that concerned Peter Monkhouse and me was the Belgian Sports Car race at Brussels in 1946. In fact there were three different races, all for sports cars, with quite a large British contingent competing. Leslie Johnson entered his BMW 328 and the Darracq that Peter and I had driven at Elstree. Then there was Pat Garland with a Sports Delage and Oscar Moore with his BMW. Neither Peter nor I went to Brussels and, it seems, we missed rather a good meeting. Charles Dunham entered his Speed 20 Alvis, to be driven by "Lofty" England; both Jock Horsfall and Tony Rolt were there with Jock's 2-litre Aston Martin. We heard all about it afterwards. Apparently, Leslie Johnson in the BMW and Jock Horsfall in the Aston Martin were the star turns in their class. In the large class, Leslie Johnson was going quite well until he had trouble with the gearbox in the Darracq.

The next race on the Continent was at Albi and I hoped I might be going with Raymond Mays and R4D, because Ray loved Albi and held the lap record there. The car was not quite ready, however, so we had to be content with hearing about it afterwards. We thought Reg Parnell would be driving the E-type ERA, but he took his Maserati instead. The only ERA competitor was "Brookie" in the old R7B, the Dobson car. Neither of them did particularly well and Nuvolari won the race quite easily in his Maserati.

The first real international Grand Prix racing after the Second World War came about a month later, at Geneva. There was a complete works entry from Alfa Romeo, with Alfa 158s, together with a full team of Maseratis from Scuderia Milano. All the top drivers were competing. We were really interested this time because Ian Connell was running his ERA and Raymond Mays had R4D. Another British entry that interested me very much was David Hampshire with the 1½-litre Delage. Bob Gerard had R14B, with a Murray-Jamieson blower instead of the Zoller. "Bira" was there with "Romulus"; before the practice session he came over to have a look at "Remus" with its crash-type gearbox, which Freddie Dixon had fitted before the war. George

Bainbridge was driving Bob Ansell's ERA and George Abecassis his Alta. The full five-car team of Alfa 158s were led by Jean-Pierre Wimille, the Maseratis by Tazio Nuvolari.

In practice, these leading Continental teams seemed to have no trouble at all; but most of the British contingent encountered every sort of problem. Ian Connell kept on cooking plugs on R5B; Raymond Mays was in and out of the pits with brake problems. As was the usual practice on the Continent, there were two heats and a final. For the first heat it was very wet. Wimille started before the flag and everyone else followed. The starter merely dropped the flag beause all the field was simply going past him. At the end of the first heat, it was Wimille and Achille Varzi in front, with no one else in sight. We were more concerned with the second heat, as Ian Connell and Raymond Mays were in it with the ERAs, as was Hampshire with his old Delage. Once again, the Alfa 158s dominated the heat. David Hampshire stalled on the line, as had so many drivers with that Delage. Ray and Ian got away very well and ran nose-to-tail for many laps, just behind George Abecassis, who was very fast indeed in the Alta. Giuseppe Farina and Count Trossi soon built up a good lead in their Alfas and they took the rest of the heat quite easily, obviously not hurrying; only Nuvolari posed any kind of threat to them. The relaxed Alfa performance was in marked contrast not only with Nuvolari, but also with the Swiss Baron Emanuel de Graffenried and, of course, the British drivers. Mays, Connell and Abecassis all tried very hard and really made no impression at all. Mays and Abecassis, however, qualified for the final.

At least as they lined up for the final, six from the first heat and six from the second, it was not raining and the track was practically dry. As with the heats, the start was a complete shambles: the first two rows started well before the drop of the flag. It seemed that the drivers on the second row did not watch for the flag, only for the tails of the front line. The first bit of drama was provided by Luigi Villoresi, who crashed and blocked the way for Reg Parnell, who also shunted, so both those cars were out. Wimille and Farina took turns to lead the race, passing and repassing, sometimes in front of the grandstand, to the great joy of the public; but I do not think they were really trying. The only person who was trying very hard was Nuvolari. Then, apparently, Nuvolari shunted into the back of Wimille, braking for a corner out of view from the grandstand and the pits. Raymond Mays only just missed that accident and over-revved in second gear, helping his brakes which were playing up. Wimille was delayed quite considerably and Nuvolari came by waving his fist. Then Wimille passed shaking his fist and Nuvolari was given the black flag. The latter took no notice at all, however, despite being shown the flag with his number lap after lap. The officials eventually put the flag away and let him get away with it. No one seemed to know whether he deserved to be black-flagged; but, in any case the public liked to see him racing, so he was allowed to carry on. "Bira" and Mays were going well, until Ray put a rod through the block, wrecking the engine, and did not finish. As expected the event finished with the Alfa 158s first, second and third – Farina, Trossi and Wimille. Nuvolari was in fourth position. The best of our crowd was "Bira" with "Romulus".

So it was that real Grand Prix racing returned to Europe. It was not much like the international Formula One events of immediately before the war, dominated as they were by the Auto Unions and Mercedes. It was more reminiscent of earlier races with the Alfa Romeos, Maseratis and Bugattis, which were great fun and very much a sport.

The differences of opinion between Humphrey Cook, Raymond Mays and Peter Berthon that had caused the split in ERA before the war were happily healed. We all lunched together at Grosvenor House and agreed that the situation had changed radically since ERA had been started in 1934 and there were now several new ways open to get Britain ahead in motor racing. For Ray and Peter, of course, there was only one way ahead and that was with the BRM.

When Humphrey Cook let it be known that he was not going to promote a Grand Prix team of his own, he said he might be

ERA E-type sports car.

interested in selling the ERA company altogether, complete with E-types. Although not yet fully developed and proved, they seemed the best bet for a British Grand Prix contender at that time. I was approached by Leslie Johnson and Laurence Pomeroy in connection with a very exciting project to buy the ERA company and produce both a sports car based on the E-type and an entirely new small saloon. They asked me if I would be prepared to join the board of directors of a new company, if they were able to obtain the necessary finance to get it off the ground. Leslie would arrange the finance and be the company chairman; "Pom" would be the technical director; I would promote and market the cars.

The proposal was to utilize the international goodwill of the ERA name, to develop a profitable home and export business in production-type cars; to make use of existing designs and equipment to produce a 2/3-seater E-type 1½-litre sports car, which would rank as one of the fastest cars in the world, would

maintain the ERA tradition and prestige and be capable of
continuing success in the field of sports car racing. It was
expected that 20 to 30 such cars could be sold per annum, at a
1939 value of £1500. Further, the plan was to design and develop
a high-grade 1100 cc saloon car capable of 80-85 mph and
35 mpg, providing a British equivalent of the technically
advanced Continental cars of that capacity. This model would
embrace proven features of Continental European design, in
respect of frame and suspension on the lines of the DKW, with
an engine somewhat similar to a Fiat and transmission of KdF
(Volkswagen) or Citröen design. Light in weight – 1790 lb was
suggested - yet with a very low centre of gravity, it was to
combine performance with comfort and stability on the road,
with special attention to be given to quiet running (this had
hitherto been regarded as a serious problem with small cars at
high speeds). It was estimated that some 4000 of such cars could
be sold at a pre-war price of £298. The plan was to acquire ERA
Limited and build the prototypes of these two models. That
would require a cash outlay of £40,000 to £50,000.

The proposers reckoned that the name of ERA and our joint
standing in the world of motor racing would create satisfactory
and confident relations with agents and dealers, ensure first-class
manufacture and service to the owners and give continuity of
policy – that is one or two models progressively improved but
basically unchanged over six to nine years. The suggestion was
that an engineering department under Pomeroy would be able to
maintain the products of the company as the best of their kind
in the world. They would locate the works so that bought-out
components would be within easy access, close to skilled labour
for assembly and near a high-speed circuit and rough

Standard 10 hp ERA saloon.

mountainous country for test purposes. They already had a location in mind. It was estimated that, to secure the objectives thoroughly and with a sales figure in excess of £100,000 (1939 value), an additional capital outlay of £150,000 would be needed.

All this seemed to be tremendously exciting. However, when I talked to Peter Berthon he said that the E-type would be impossible as a sports car and, in any case, needed drastic development, which he alone fully understood because he had been responsible for the original design. He claimed that the continuous trouble with the E-type could have been solved "ages

ERA 10 hp aerodynamic saloon, capable of 90 mph.

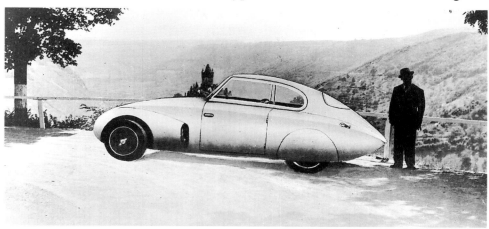

ago" if he had been allowed to develop the car as originally planned.

Leslie and "Pom" believed that the E-type sports car was a viable proposition and that it would appeal to wealthy sportsmen. They reckoned that it would be unbeatable in the 1½-litre class for some years, as well as being a strong challenger regardless of engine size. They were of the opinion that a detuned engine with a 2/3-seater body fully equipped should well exceed 130 mph on pump fuel, with only reasonable modifications. The Zoller compressor would be removed and a Roots-type fitted, blowing at about 10 lb, giving 140-150 bhp at 7500 rpm. The gear lever and steering system would be changed from central to righthand-drive position, or to lefthand drive if required. They reckoned that the 1939 value with an open body would be £1500. Suspension would be trailing link i.f.s. at the front with laminated torsion bars and a dead axle with transverse leafspring at the rear. There would be Armstrong hydraulic shock absorbers; hydraulic brakes, operating two leading shoes in 11 in cast-iron drums; a backbone type tubular frame with cross tubes for body mounting; while a very special low-drag body was envisaged. Accessories would be a Delco electrical system, AC pump, SU carburettors and Michelin wheels and tyres. Leslie and "Pom" gave me a large, 40-page brochure, which went into great detail with regard to the design and the possibilities of this project, forecasts and every sort of graph and information.

We studied this together in some detail and I gave them the answer that I would be most interested in joining such a project. Apparently, I was given this opportunity of joining the new company because of my promotion of the "Rembrandt" meetings and getting the sport going again after the war.

After some weeks of negotiation, a price was agreed for the sale of the ERA company with the existing cars and it was left that Leslie Johnson would go into the matter of raising that sum of money. In the meantime, of course, it was understood that we would keep this to ourselves and that I certainly would not show the brochure or tell anyone about the project until it was decided to go ahead.

The project was the subject of many meetings over a year or so. Leslie bought the ERA company and made many attempts to get the bugs out of the E-types, but with little success. There were several likely financiers for the sports car project, but nothing came of it. One of the problems was that the estimates for the amount of capital required kept on increasing all the time.

I personally liked everything about the project and would have loved to have worked with Leslie and "Pom", because we three had an excellent rapport. Looking back on the project, after some 40 years, I think Peter Berthon was right: his E-type racing car required a basic redesign and, even if after that it was successful, it would never have been a good basis for a sports car.

The 1100 cc saloon car could have been a winner, I believe, because it was not until Alec Issigonis' Morris Minor appeared in 1950 that Britain had an outstanding small saloon.

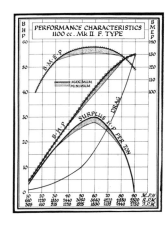 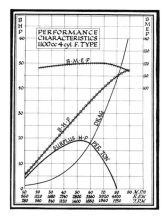

CHAPTER FOURTEEN

The time had come to consider our plans for 1947. I loved the little "Hurg". It was great fun on the road and on the track, but I had my sights on something rather quicker. Before the war, I had been rather spoiled by driving much faster and more exotic racing cars owned by other people, so now I wanted a real racing car of my own. At the Monaco works we had been looking after the single-seater N-type MG Magnette that Donald Pitt had been racing. This was the ex-John Dugdale car that I had always admired. After John Dugdale, this car had been driven by my friends Mike Edmundson and Tony Hurst, who had put up some fine performances at Brooklands. Now, Donald Pitt was buying a Lester MG for longer-distance sports car events and was selling the Magnette. Donald's price was £750, a lot of money in those days, but quite fair. I knew that the car was in good condition, as we had done all the preparation ourselves.

I reckoned that I would get nearly half that price for the HRG, but even then I could not really afford the Magnette. Donald had someone else quite interested, so I decided that I would have to forget that sort of car for some time. Then Leslie Johnson and his wife came over for dinner one evening. Leslie asked what my plans were for the next season, saying "Rivers, I would like to see you in something faster than the HRG". I told him about the single-seater MG Magnette, but said that I would have to wait another year before I could afford it. Leslie Johnson simply wrote a cheque for £750 and handed it over, saying, "This is not a loan: it is a present". Before I could find any words, he said, "You can pay me back one day, if you find you can do it easily; and, if you can't then this is a gift". He went on to say, "I have enough money and I want you to have that MG".

Penny and I were flabbergasted. People just do not do such things, not even very rich people – in fact, especially not very rich people! We argued about it, but Leslie was adamant. In the end, I took his cheque and bought the Magnette. Some months later, I repaid him £300 when I sold the HRG; but it was nearly two years before I paid him the rest. He refused any interest. What can you say of such a man? Such generosity – and I know that he was equally generous to other people as well.

The Magnette was sitting in our racing shop at Monaco, all ready for the next season's racing, but I decided to get it home. Of course I wanted to look at it, sit in it and familiarize myself with every bit of it. It was very exciting, having your own first racing car! Driving other people's racing cars has some obvious advantages, but there is nothing like the pleasure of possession. The decision to have the Magnette was influenced by the fact that we had acquired that very good amateur, unpaid mechanic, Ronnie Mountford. Ronnie enthusiastically agreed to take charge of the preparation of the Magnette. We were joined by another friend and his wife, Charles and Eva Meisl, whom we had met at one of the "Rembrandt" meetings. Charles, a Czechoslovakian who had served in the RAF during the war, owned an Alvis 12/50. We five decided to form our own équipe and planned a full season of racing events for the year.

My first drive in the Magnette was at Cockfosters, on the private roads of the building site near Barnet where we had organized the first postwar event in 1945. We had detachable wings and a Brooklands silencer on the Magnette and the car rode behind our works Standard on a fixed tow bar. Ronnie sat in the Magnette and steered and also assisted with the braking when required. Sometimes we used trade plates and, in one way or another, we thought it was all very nearly legal!

Policemen were always interested and very helpful in fact, despite some rather doubtful aspects of our entourage. For our first trial run, Peter Monkhouse and his chief mechanic, Jack Jaggard, mixed up some 80/10/10 Pool petrol, Benzol and Methanol and we used a set of very soft Lodge plugs. Peter reckoned that the needles of the SU carburettors were not too far out. They would probably be good enough until his friend, Ian MacLachlan, who was an expert on such things, could decide on the best fuel and needles.

There was no self-starter, of course, so it was very useful having the racing car on a fixed tow bar to get it going. It fired quickly and Ronnie warmed it up before I did a few runs on our circuit. The engine note was never quite clean, although we changed several plugs. There were no problems with the gear change, which was very quick indeed with the close-ratio box.

We returned the car to the Monaco works the next day and Peter altered the needles a little. I took the car up the road on trade plates and it seemed better, but there was neither the time nor the opportunity for a proper test before our first event, the Cofton Hackett Sprint at Longbridge, run by the MMEC and SUNBAC.

I had of course driven a lot of racing cars for other people, mostly on test at Brooklands and Donington and many of these machines were much faster than my Magnette. On those occasions, however, someone else had done all the work, made all the decisions and borne the responsibility. Now it was quite different. It was my own car, I was entering it and it was the Rivers Fletcher équipe that was responsible. All very exciting. Ronnie came over to Monaco at Watford on Friday afternoon and checked everything. Peter Monkhouse had a last look at the car, inspected all the plugs in their boxes and told Ronnie which

On test on the Watford bypass, young Peter in the cockpit.

were to be used for warming up and which for racing.

Charles and Eva were going separately in the Alvis from their flat in Hampstead, so we arranged a rendezvous at Longbridge for 10.30 am on the Saturday. On the run to the event, the poor old Standard coped very well, but it was a heavy load and the slightest upgrade brought us down to third, often to second, gear. The weather was fine and we had the sunshine roof open. I rather envied Ronnie in the fresh air in the Magnette. We called at a welcome coffee stop in open country and made two more stops for the usual reason. There was another stop to wire up the front wings on the Magnette, because a wing stay had fractured. Ronnie diagnosed the reason as the hard ride of the suspension, so he slacked off the shock absorbers, a procedure that we adopted with success for the rest of the season. He straight away added a warning note that we should make sure that we tightened the shockers before the start of any practice run or racing. These notes were part of the routine checklist and log which were all included in the équipe plan.

Ronnie, having been at Austin at Longbridge, knew the way to Cofton Hackett. It used to be the Austin test track. Charles and Eva were already there and had found our place in the paddock. To our great relief, the scrutineer found nothing to complain of and congratulated Ronnie on the turn-out. This was well deserved because he had been to a lot of trouble making sure that everything was right, tight and scrupulously clean. We were soon joined by our friends Doug and Mavis Chamberlain, from Henley-in-Arden, with whom we were staying the night. There were many more friends to greet in the paddock: Reg Parnell with an ERA; Bob and Joan Gerard with a Riley; Barry Woodall with one of the Chula-modified 1½-litre Delages; and Ted Lund with an MG. In fact, we seemed to know most people there because nearly everyone had been to our "Rembrandt" meetings.

While Penny and I were socializing, Ronnie and Charles were warming up the Magnette and already seemed to have problems. They could not keep the plugs clean. Whatever Ronnie did and however many times he cleaned them, the plugs kept oiling up. It was very tiresome, but we thought that when we did get the engine really hot there should not be a problem. So, after a lot of popping and banging, we got the temperature up. Then it was helmet and goggles on for a practice run. A push-start from Ronnie and Charles and she started away, firing on all six. It sounded fine and I got away well; but at nearly full revs, about 6500, I lost a cylinder and then another one, so came back to our stall in the paddock on about three cylinders. Ronnie spat on his fingers, felt all the plugs and found three definitely colder than the rest, which he quickly replaced with new ones.

Ronnie adds a little oil.

Off I went on my second run, with just the same result but not on all the same cylinders. Examination of the electrodes suggested that we were cooking them, whereas earlier we had been wetting them. Ronnie had a look at the carburettors; they seemed fine and he wondered if the mixture was too weak. I went twice more up and down the paddock, but still the chronic misfiring. It was an absolute mystery, as the Magnette had been so much better when I had taken it out on the previous day at Watford.

Peter Monkhouse was not racing that day, but he said he would come over to see how we were doing in the afternoon. We had tried and checked everything and felt completely lost, when Peter suddenly appeared. "You great fools", he exclaimed, "you are warming up on the hard plugs and trying to race on the soft ones! I told you which plugs to use, why didn't you take notice?"

Of course, somehow or other, Ronnie had got them the wrong way round. As I have said before, the Monkhouses do not suffer fools gladly. With the right set of plugs for warming up and the right ones for racing, everything was fine; well certainly much better. There was no misfiring and the car felt quite good, although not giving as much power as it really should. Reg Parnell made the fastest time of the day in the ERA, and we were very pleased to see Donald Pitt fastest in his class in his new Lester MG. It had been a good day and we all learned a few things: most important was the fact that we all felt we were going to have a lot of fun running the Magnette.

On the outward journey we had encountered no steep hills. On our return on Sunday, however, after leaving Henley-in-Arden and Stratford-upon-Avon, we had to surmount the edge of the Cotswolds, namely Sunrising Hill. This famous test hill of the 1920s, now on a good main road, brought the Standard Ten down to a crawl in first gear. Very soon it felt as though we

Leaving the S-bends at Prescott, 1947.

might not reach the top. Ronnie summed up the situation in a flash and, in the cockpit of the Magnette, he turned on the fuel, switched the ignition on and engaged second gear. The racing car fired straight away. With the fixed tow bar, we immediately received a hefty push. It was completely unrehearsed, but a brilliant performance from Ronnie. You can imagine my astonishment, receiving this terrific boost just when I feared that we were about to stall! Ronnie's grin and thumbs up signal

Prescott scene: practice, with Bob Gerard's ERA being started on the handle.

reassured us and our two-headed caravan roared over the crest of Sunrising to the accompaniment of the healthy roar of the unsilenced racing car's exhaust.

Our next event was Prescott which was several weeks away. Peter Monkhouse said he would take the engine down. He was convinced that there was a lot more power somewhere. He found that the valve springs had lost their temper, so he fitted a new set of the same type that he had used in his racing P-type at Brooklands. Peter and Ian MacLachlan considered that the 80/10/10 fuel probably made the engine run too hot and might burn the pistons. Mac consequently brewed up a special fuel: 50 per cent methanol, 20 per cent benzol, 8 per cent acetone, 6 per cent nitro-benzene, 8 per cent Pool petrol and 8 per cent petrol-ether. He also made up some new needles for the carburettors.

Testing showed this to be very much better. The ignition was clean all the way, the engine ran cooler and there was a lot more power. We had good friends with a spray shop close to our Monaco works. They resprayed the Magnette in my special shade of blue, just as they had done with the HRG. All was set now for the Bugatti Owners' Club beginning of the season testing weekend. Here, the car ran very well and we all had great fun. This used to be a most enjoyable event and very useful but, alas, it is no longer on the club's calendar.

In my book *MG – Past and Present*, I detailed the four seasons we had with that Magnette. It will therefore suffice here to record that we ran the car in nearly every event it was eligible for, had a great deal of enjoyment, but no real success. The car handled well but was not really competitive; it did not have quite enough power and, of course, I was no potential ace driver either! Circuit racing at Gransden Lodge was more fun with the Magnette than I had found with the HRG, but again I was unplaced.

At this time I also drove several other cars including a very good supercharged AC.

Peter Monkhouse and I attended the Ministry of Civil Aviation Light Aircraft Meeting at White Waltham on 18 June 1947. Our Monaco aero-engine was not ready, but we flew in a Chrislea Ace, which was the plane destined for our power unit.

On the line at Gransden Lodge.

Later in the day we met the Alvis driver, Michael May, who asked us if we would like a ride with him in his own aircraft, (I cannot remember what type it was). It was a nice little three-seater which seemed to go well. After flying around for a while, Michael asked us if it was all right to land. Neither Peter nor I had any notion of the arrangements and there did seem to be an awful lot of planes buzzing around. We assumed that Michael knew the drill. He, however, said he was a newcomer, that this was his first plane, he had only just got his pilot's licence and he had assumed that we would know everything because we were aero-engine builders.

It all looked somewhat dangerous to me. Michael asked us, "What do you think those signals on the ground mean? Why is that chap waving a flag?" Planes were taking off and landing and, presumably, everyone else knew what they were up to. When there seemed to be a lull in the proceedings we had a quick look all round and then zoomed down. There was not much of a bump and Michael taxied off the runway as quickly as possible. Peter and I were very relieved to be safely on the ground once more. A knowledgeable pilot of a twin-engined plane came over and thanked Michael for giving him plenty of space. "Not at all, old chap, a pleasure", replied Michael, who of course had not seen him at all! It was an exciting day and set me to wondering if light aircraft would be part of my life in the future.

The Chrislea Ace at White Waltham.

CHAPTER FIFTEEN

The ERA Club decided that, because of the changed situation, the club should be closed down. The funds were used to make a fine model ERA, which was presented to the British Racing Drivers' Club. The model, which was made by Rex Hayes, has become a major BRDC trophy. The first winners were Jock Horsfall and Leslie Johnson. Over the years many of the top drivers have won this trophy, including Mike Hawthorn, Ron Flockhart, Stirling Moss, Jack Brabham, Roy Salvadori, Graham Hill, Jim Clark and Brian Redman.

We really loved the MG Magnette and decided to keep it after the first two seasons, but we considered how we could improve its performance for 1949. "It's quite easy: the car is far too big and heavy", said Peter Monkhouse. "We will shorten the chassis, throw away the huge fuel tank and put a little 2-or 3-gallon tank beside the driver and make up a short new light tail". Peter and I crawled all over the car, measured everything and I made some drawings. We took my drawings to John Wyer, who was in charge of the car business at Watford. One look and he told us that he thought we were mad: he said such a car would never handle and would be lethal.

I had great faith in Peter, who disagreed with John, but I listened to both opinions. Peter really was a brilliant engineer and he had been so right in so many important and different engineering problems at Monaco, that I had no hesitation in deciding to go his way. After much discussion, John Wyer said he would carry out the rebuild, but he considered that we were absolutely wrong in thinking that the car would handle at all if it was shortened in that way. They made a beautiful job of it and I was delighted with the car when it was finished, because it looked rather like a little ERA. Peter took it out on the road, but we had new pistons so he could not drive very fast. Obviously, it needed some running in, despite the fact that we had used racing clearances. He considered that the car was satisfactory, while John Wyer shook his head sadly. I then drove it around the de Havilland airfield for about half an hour fairly slowly and at that speed I thought and felt it was fine.

Our first event with the shortened MG was a sprint at Silverstone. By that time our tow car was not the Standard Ten, but the ex-Marcus Chambers Riley Nine Monaco saloon of 1933 I had bought. Ronnie could not make it for that event and Charles and Eva were abroad, so my young brother Michael came along with us, steering the Magnette on tow. In practice, the engine tightened up and almost seized when I gave it anything like full revs. Humphrey Cook's old mechanic, Pugh, was with us at Monaco at that time and he came along to give us a hand. There was plenty of time before the racing began so we decided to withdraw a piston to have a look. We turned the car over on its side: this did look rather horrifying, but in fact that was the easiest way to do the job. All we had to do was to drain the fuel and oil, which was quite straightforward. As soon as we withdrew one piston, we saw that they were far too tight and there was no chance of racing until we had fully run in the car.

I was still happy and confident about the whole project and, after careful and complete running in, everything looked good for

our first Prescott hillclimb with the short-chassis Magnette. Taking it quite carefully up for my first practice run, I nevertheless spun it at Orchard, lost it in the S-bends and got it sideways on the semicircle! Ronnie checked everything and had a good look round before I had another go. Perhaps I was being too careful: would it handle better if I gave it some stick? Leaving Orchard with tyres smoking, I left the road on the inside of the bend and hit a tree quite hard, banging my head on the screen and bending the tie bar between the dove irons. I reversed slowly back to the start at the paddock, a bit shattered. We checked everything and, after straightening the tie bar, I did manage to complete another practice run without spinning or hitting anything; but it was hard work and my time was very slow.

For the next Prescott, we considered the situation. It seemed that we were a good deal faster on the getaway and while going straight, but the car would not answer to the helm on the corners. We tried every variation on shock absorbers, adjustments and tyre pressures to no avail. It looked as though John Wyer

Above:
"Pom" and Elsa Pomeroy opening a Prescott meeting in the Prince Henry Vauxhall designed by Pomeroy's father.

Above left:
The MG Magnette on its side at Silverstone – the easiest way to spot the trouble.

had been right – it just would not handle. Every practice run was hopeless.

On the day I got it nearly right at Orchard Corner, with a lot of opposite lock; then, at Pardon Hairpin, the car tipped up, very nearly overturning, so a very chastened Rivers Fletcher completed the rest of the meeting at a dismally slow pace. Great Auclum was the next event and it was not quite so bad. Perhaps I was getting the hang of it! Anyway, I stormed round the top of the banking as if I was John Cobb on the Napier-Railton at Brooklands and put up a good fast time. However, I was getting a bit frightened and kept thinking of the hereafter. Cheerful friends asked about my choice of flowers and kept asking if I had remembered to make a will!

Luton Hoo, with George Hartwell on the line with the Monaco 500. Behind the car: Clive Gallop, Ron Godfrey, Kent Karslake, Mac McKenzie; on this side of the car, Peter Monkhouse looks critically at his creation.

Back at the works, Peter was still full of confidence. He said all we needed to do was to fit smaller wheels and big tyres at the rear to restore the balance. He convinced me that this would be right; so we got new wheels and big "boots" and set off for the next Prescott with renewed confidence. On my first practice run, I certainly made a demon getaway and achieved a very hairy Orchard Corner and Pardon Hairpin, before spinning round twice in the S-bends, miraculously missing everything – banks, barriers and trees.

At the Brighton Speed Trials everything was fine and the car ran very well – but of course this was only a straight sprint. We ran the car in another sprint at Tewin Water and Penny made her début in that event, driving the Magnette. We had a good day and I won my class. Penny was "fastest lady", winning a nice cup and beating Colin Chapman's girlfriend Hazel (later his wife), who drove Colin's Austin Special.

At the end of the event there was an amusing incident when Penny was driving back down the course on our tender Riley. She forgot that my cousin Richard was holding the end of the tow bar still fixed on the tail of the Riley. She sped down the course with poor Richard, taking ever longer strides, touching the ground at long intervals, trying to keep pace with the Riley. He

only just made it. The spectators loved it, but Penny was
horrified afterwards, realizing that she could so easily have
brought him down heavily.

As motor racing consultant to Gainsborough Films, later part
of MGM, I had some good jobs at the studios at Elstree and
Denham. One day, I had a panic telephone call from the
producer of the film *Pandora and the Flying Dutchman*, starring
James Mason and Ava Gardner. He told me that they had some
sequences of Nigel Patrick driving the Napier-Railton and,
somehow or other, they were lacking any sound track of the
noise of the car. The film was to be "put in the can", as they
term it, within two days. Could I bring a suitable racing car to a
nearby venue, so that the noise of the car warming up, racing,
cornering, skidding and having a pit stop could be recorded? The
producer said it had to be that very afternoon or, at the latest,

the next day. I told him it was impossible at such short notice.
He said that it did not matter what it cost, it had to be done. I
would have to go immediately to the studios, see the shots and
time the sequences so that sound could be recorded without
delay.

The only racing car that could be run at that moment at
Monaco was my Magnette: hardly ideal since its 1100 cc and
6 cylinders would have to pretend to be 24 litres and 12
cylinders. I told the producer that I thought it would do. "Jolly
good: go ahead", he said. I raced over to the studio and, in the
meantime, gave instructions for the Magnette to be prepared.
Ronnie Mountford was too far away in Bournemouth, so I rang
my friend Kenneth Brown at Barnet, who was fortunately
available to mechanic for me. The next morning, Kenneth and I
took the Magnette to Finmere airfield, where we met the
producer of the film and Celia, who was the stand-in for Ava
Gardner. We were soon followed by the sound crew. I sped up
and down the runway for hours and slid round in circles to
provide the squeal of tyres for cornering. Kenneth knocked the
hubs off and on and threw spanners around to simulate a pit
stop. The whole thing was a riot: we were most amused and the
producer was delighted.

Somewhat to our amazement, the final production of *Pandora
and the Flying Dutchman* was a very good film, although to the
knowledgeable enthusiast the motor racing sequences were a bit
of a giggle. Thankfully, the Napier-Railton that went over the
edge of a cliff was only a mock-up. Strangely enough no one,

Above:

*Nearly over but not quite!
Signalling intending to turn
right – the author has
certainly turned quite far
enough to the left. Autocar.*

Above left:

*High on the banking at Great
Auclum on the shortened MG
Magnette.*

not even the experts, made any adverse comments on the car noise. More recently, the film was revived on television and I enjoyed it again. Our friends, who knew of the Magnette intrusion, laughed with us; but even now the noise does not sound very out of place.

Our next event should have been Shelsley Walsh, but I funked it, believing that I would have an almighty shunt if I tried it at all. We did one more Prescott, which was very dicey. On my last run, really trying, I came into the S-bends quite fast – but backwards! John Bolster happened to be watching at that point and he came up to me afterwards saying, "Rivers, if you don't get rid of that Magnette, it will surely get rid of you". That was it and I parted with a car that I loved first of all but then spoiled.

The Magnette later appeared in Ireland, where someone fitted an even heavier 2.5-litre MG engine. It must have been impossible to handle, and the owner confessed to me that he only used it in straight-line sprints. However, another great enthusiast in Belfast, Henry Corry, has now bought the car and is correcting our faults by having the chassis rebuilt to the original length. With that big job being expertly handled by Brown and

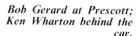

Bob Gerard at Prescott; Ken Wharton behind the car.

Gammons, and the rest of the car completely restored, the N-type Magnette originally built for John Dugdale and later owned and loved by Mike Edmondson and me, should be back on the circuits again.

While we were having a lot of fun with our Magnette, my Canadian friend Frank Kennington had real success with his two MG K3s. One was a 1933 Mille Miglia slab-tank model, the other a 1934 long-tailed car. Frank was very successful with those in hillclimbs and at Goodwood. Another very successful MG driver at that time was Ted Lund from the North of England. I had got to know him when he came to the "Rembrandt" meetings, and he was one of the very few people who used a racing Q-type on the road before the war. That must have been quite something: the Q-types had terrific performance, but all of them were extremely noisy, so I wonder how he managed to avoid silencer problems. Another great friend of ours was Ernie Robb, in Belfast. He bought an MG J4 from us at Monaco and proceeded to win nearly everything in sight. In its class, the J4 was almost unbeatable and at the Craigantlet hillclimb before the war he won six classes and made second best time to Bert Hadley in the works Austin. Sewell, Austin's competition manager, was so impressed that he invited Robb to join the Austin works team. The outbreak of war put paid to that project and, after the war, with no works Austins running, Ernie Robb had it all his own way in Northern Ireland.

Peter Monkhouse married his secretary, Peggy Candy. There were only five of us present, including Ian MacLachlan and Peggy's actress sister, Kath. After the registry office ceremony the wedding breakfast was at an hotel on the A5, the old Watling Street.

After quite a lot of champagne the party posed round the Bugatti Type 51 which Peter had insisted on using for the wedding. I took the photos which, sadly, were to be the very last

picture of the famous club car. Against all our urgent advice, Peter set off with Kath, not with his just-married wife Peggy, promising Kath they would achieve a "ton" on the open road.

Peggy, Ian MacLachlan, the other guests and I followed in MacLachlan's MG. Already I was fearful of the situation. Cresting a hill on Watling Street, we were horrified to see the Bugatti in bits all over the road, a smashed-up lorry, Kath lying

Going well at the Brighton Speed Trials, beating Blomfield's Bugatti Type 37.

face-down on the road and Peter struggling to get out of the ditch.

It looked just about as bad as it could be, because the Bugatti had hit the lorry head-on at full speed. Kath was severely injured, Peter had many bruises and a broken ankle, but the lorry driver was unhurt. The Bugatti was a write-off, although the engine and some bits were salvaged later.

That night, Peter on crutches and a very shaken Peggy, with her wedding outfit spattered with blood where she had attended to her injured sister, spent the first night of their married life – not on speaking terms – in our double bed at "Noddings".

Above:
Last picture of the Club Bugatti. The newly-weds, Peter and Peggy, kiss before Peter races off in the Bugatti with Peggy's sister Kath. Both Ian McLachlan behind the car and the Bugatti are wearing their wedding carnations.

Above right:

On location at Finmere airfield for the film, *Pandora and the Flying Dutchman:* **Kenneth Brown, Celia (stand-in for Ava Gardner) and Richard Booth.**

In fact, Peter and Peggy had to spend the rest of their honeymoon in our house so that we could all make daily visits to Kath in Luton hospital. Not a good beginning, but Peter and Peggy made it up and Kath made a good recovery.

Police proceedings were serious and insurance very costly. With difficulty, I managed not to be subpoenaed to appear at court, and Peter managed to retain his driving licence and the fine was not too crippling.

CHAPTER SIXTEEN

With war contracts coming to an end, London Aircraft
Productions Company was closed; so that was the end of most of
our business with AEC. My opposite number at Southall was Mr
Still, the production controller of AEC. He was a brilliant man
who, with his many new production ideas, increased the output
of AEC and all its subsidiaries considerably. He helped me a
great deal over the years and I owe him a lot for his skill and
patience. Now AEC was returning to building London buses and
commercial vehicles, so he and I turned our production at Kings
Langley in a different direction.

This was very successful and we even put on a night shift to
cope with more work for Crossley at Manchester, a firm that was
collaborating closely with AEC making buses for the North of
England. Despite the excellent revenue this brought in we were
never able to keep up with the escalating cost of development of
our aero-engine.

On occasions, I used a vintage sports car that we were working
on and testing at Monaco for my visits to Southall. One day,
when I arrived in Peter Monkhouse's Alfa Romeo coupé, Lord
Brabazon was present and insisted on having a short drive
himself.

At Kings Langley there was excitement when the aero-engine
ran for the first time, quite promisingly, spinning a prop on loan
from de Havilland. That was real progress – but our company
was getting further and further into the red. It was just as
"Brab" had warned. After several months of desperate
negotiations with our bank, one Monday morning Peter
Monkhouse came into my office and said that he was sorry, but
we were finished. He had tried everything, but the bank would
not honour our cheque for the wages for that Friday. He looked
awful, absolutely all in. Poor Peter had been so enthusiastic
about the engine and certainly put his heart into the project.
Peggy was in tears and I felt desperately sorry for both of them.

I had only one thought in mind and I asked Peter if I could
go and see "Brab". Although he hated the idea, because "Brab"
had warned him several times, Peter agreed, saying that he would

leave it to me. I got through to Lord Brabazon straight away, asking him for an urgent meeting. I think he must have guessed what was happening, because he said he would meet me at AEC at Southall the next morning. AEC paid the wages on Friday; but, of course, Peter knew that he had lost the company.

The next few weeks were filled with meetings between Peter Monkhouse, Lord Brabazon and other directors of AEC and then there were further meetings with the directors of Chrislea Aircraft. The eventual result of all those negotiations and investigations into the aero-engine project was very sad for Peter. It was decided that the aero-engine was not a commercial proposition, for even if it had been right first time without serious modifications or development, which would have been unlikely, there was an insufficient requirement for the engine.

No longer only for the few—the Air is now Everyman's Highway

MONACO

LIGHT *British* AERO ENGINES

75 *and* 100 H.P.

Above left:
The Monaco aero-engine runs for the first time, spinning a prop borrowed from de Havilland.

Above right:
Monaco catalogue.

Peter's scheme was a brave project, which really deserved a better fate. No one blamed him but, as it turned out, there was no postwar rush to buy light aircraft after all. The great demand was for cars and it was the old garage business at Watford, which Ian Connell had carried on as before, that prospered while Peter's new aero-engine company went to the wall.

For some time Monaco continued to do subcontract work for AEC, but eventually the factory became a company within the Associated Commercial Vehicles Limited Group, making bearings for the whole group.

Peter had been the main shareholder and I only had a nominal stake as a director. There were no hard feelings and I was given a reasonable payment for my negotiations. Peter resigned from the garage business, too, formed another small company with Peggy and took time to consider future products.

One-make clubs were starting to appear. Although only a few ERAs were competing in important races, a lot of them were driven in the big hillclimbs at Shelsley Walsh and Prescott. We therefore decided to resurrect the ERA Club, not as we had run it before the war supporting the works, but like other one-make clubs helping the owners to help one another. The old firm of Mays, Cook and Berthon came to another inaugural meeting and Barry Eastick did a great job as secretary.

To encourage the new owners, Raymond Mays gave a trophy for the fastest time by an ERA at Shelsley Walsh and I gave a similar trophy for the fastest at Prescott.

On a visit to Bourne, Raymond Mays gave the exciting news that his British Racing Motors project was definitely on and getting a good start. Two leading industrialists, Oliver Lucas for Joseph Lucas, makers of electrical components and Alfred Owen for Rubery Owen, one of the largest groups of engineering companies, had each given £1000 and the promise of free manufacturing of parts to get it started. Ray was overjoyed and was confident that, with such a fine start, he would get the rest of the backing required. He said to me, "I am sure we will be together in BRM in due course and we will beat the world".

Just as ERA had been part of my life before the war, I felt that BRM should be the same now. I was most happy and relaxed with that team, where I felt I belonged. Already I could see how it would be, so like the old firm of ERA. Life with BRM at Bourne, or wherever it was racing, would no doubt revolve around Raymond Mays. He was the star personality; he knew it and everyone accepted it. Like one of his great friends in the theatre, Ivor Novello, he was surrounded and spoiled by countless friends and relatives. Each had burning enthusiasm.

Ray, tall, handsome and distinguished, was always immaculately dressed in pale blue silk shirt and tie, whether in sports clothes or in a city suit. His manners were exquisite, his conversation was stylized with extravagant phraseology: "darlings", "dearests", and "duckies" were "fantastic", "terrific" and "wizard". But above all else Ray had style.

His close friends, those of both sexes who shared his confidence, were all "special" to him. For him his friends were always right, whether, in fact, they were right or wrong. This facet of his friendship could be embarrassing, because most of us are not able to return such unswerving and sometimes unreasonable loyalty. That was how Raymond Mays was before the war and I could see that he would be just the same with BRM. He was already building the same team, for Peter Berthon was going to be the designer of the BRM.

Peter, of medium height and rather stocky build, had been quite incredibly good-looking as a young man, was still very attractive and able to charm the birds out of the trees: any bird out of any tree. He shared Ray's extravagant phraseology, but not quite to the same extent. He was very quick witted and his repartee, particularly with Ray, was always amusing. I reckoned that Peter's time-keeping would be just as chaotic with BRM as it used to be at ERA, but I knew that his brilliance as an innovative engineer could be very worthwhile.

Eastgate House at Bourne was a Georgian family residence owned by the Mays family for generations. In Ray's youth there had been a reasonable amount of garden and a tennis court, an orchard, ample stabling and garages for half a dozen cars. In the 1930s, ERA had encroached considerably; now the plans for BRM meant that precious little garden would be left.

The hierarchy of Eastgate House was well-established –
attended by a bevy of maiden aunts, a house-keeper, a cook; but
now with war-time restrictions only one housemaid, no "tweeny"
and only one gardener. Raymond Mays' devoted private secretary
'Trishie' married and retired; now a new private secretary, Miss
Ingleby was in situ. I could see that BRM at Bourne would be
likely to be a most attractive and enjoyable situation and hoped
that I could one day be part of it; not yet, there was nothing for
me at that time, but perhaps one day in the future.

Wonderful enthusiasm, it was great to see and share it. Mays
was right, quite right, but it took sixteen years and all the
enthusiasm in the world to achieve it, not only Ray's enthusiasm,
faith and drive, but the same for his partner, Peter Berthon and
one of the original backers, Alfred Owen, who eventually owned
and controlled BRM. That was the way ahead, many frustrating
miles ahead, not only for Raymond Mays, Peter Berthon and
Alfred Owen and of course for their co-directors, managers,
workers, drivers and mechanics, but most of all for their families
who eventually had to share the criticisms and responsibility of
BRM. On that day in 1946 having coffee after lunch at Eastgate
House I could only share Ray's enthusiasm and believe that it
could be done. That very night he was going off to Sheffield to
talk with leaders in the Sheffield steel industry, hoping to enlist
their help. Not surprisingly he got it and over the years he talked
and talked to countless companies and every sort of audience
with his infectious enthusiasm.

With the end of Monaco Engines Limited, I was very worried
about my own immediate future. Lord Brabazon called me to a
meeting at his London office and said that he was not sure my
future was with a group of companies making buses and
commercial vehicles. He told me I should be a public relations
officer. I asked him what that was and he explained that this was
a new idea, started in America. He said that all the big American
corporations had PROs, and he was convinced that all the big
British motor companies would need them to get ahead in world
markets. He said I was in a splendid position to promote
companies involved with sports and racing cars, just as I had
promoted the sport during the war. He said, "Set yourself up as
a public relations consultant and I'll help you". He explained
that a PRO was more than a publicity or advertising manager,
but should be responsible for that as well as promoting the
activities of the company in the sphere of its own staff and
workers, customers and suppliers.

It all sounded very exciting and promising, but I explained to
"Brab" that I had no capital at all and was entirely dependent
on a regular salary to provide for my wife and baby son. I told
him that I was in no position to be self-employed. "Brab" tried
to persuade me and eventually he said, "I want you to do it, and
I'll give you the first nine months' work at your present salary
and all expenses paid".

Of course, that was a wonderful offer and I could not refuse
it, but I was rather scared. He said that my first job for him
would not be normal public relations, but it would be interesting
and exciting and would give him a clear indication of my
abilities. He would not say any more, but told me that he would

give me full details in a week's time. I drove home in a daze, feeling that I was very fortunate but only vaguely confident that, somehow or other, it would prove to be all right. It turned out that the AEC, Maudslay and Crossley companies were now combined as ACV, Associated Commercial Vehicles Limited. Each company made buses and commercial vehicles, with their own engines, chassis, gearboxes and bodies and each had its own drawing offices, sales and other departments. I was required to spend three months in each firm, where I would be shown everything and given access to all departments, figures, company history and so on. Then I was to submit a confidential report to the directors of ACV, recommending how the group should be reconstructed, allocating manufacturing and other activities so that the products of the separate companies would not be in competition with one another.

I thought this was a great but daunting opportunity. I discussed it with my friends – Peter Monkhouse, who thought it was right up my street and quite straightforward and Peter Berthon, who was equally enthusiastic but considered that I would find it terribly difficult.

Over the previous years, I had seen a great deal of Laurence Pomeroy, technical editor of *Motor*, who had been such a help with the organization of the "Rembrandt" meetings and George Monkhouse, chief engineer of the Kodak Company, Peter's cousin, who had also assisted me greatly with these gatherings. I consulted them and they both agreed to lend a hand. They were indeed both of great material help, particularly in the compilation of my final report.

I started with AEC, where I already had many friends; then after the first three months I went to stay in Stratford-upon-Avon to spend my second stint with Castle Maudslay at Alcester; finally going to Crossley at Manchester. Before I had completed my time at Manchester, ACV purchased another company for the group, Park Royal Vehicles at Acton. I therefore spent a complete year on this interesting project for Lord Brabazon. I think that perhaps the most interesting part for me and the work I was best suited for, was in connection with the coachbuilding activities of the various companies (particularly at Crossleys, for this firm had previously built the bodies for its private cars). I drove many large vehicles, including quite a considerable mileage at the wheel of automatic gear-changing buses with the Brockhouse Salerni system, long before automatic gearboxes were generally available.

My final report, carefully edited by "Pom", was well received but I knew that my future would not be with the ACV group.

"Brab" called me to his office again and told me that he had another job for me, but this time it could be a permanent appointment. He was a director of the Tilling Group, which included Daimler Hire in London. He wanted me to take over the job of sales manager of the latter firm. He said that in due course I should be the PRO of Tilling, but the group was not quite ready for that sort of appointment and this would be a good start. It sounded fine: I would be based in London, well-paid, and with "Brab" behind me. To clinch the deal, I only had to attend a meeting with "Brab" and the chairman of the Tilling

Group, Lionel Frazer, at Crewe House in Curzon Street. I thought the meeting went very well and the chairman was very charming. We went through the preliminaries and then he raised the question of my interest in motor racing. I well knew that Daimler Hire had no connection with the sport at all, so I reckoned that this was a tricky question. I dismissed my interest in the sport as merely peripheral, explaining that it was only to enable me to make contact with persons and companies of commercial value to a business. That sounded fairly convincing, so I warmed to my subject, claiming how I saw the sport as a useful "entrée" to business.

"Brab" said nothing and the meeting ended quite cordially. When I returned home I told Penny that I thought it was all very promising, in that I had put up a good show explaining that my line was very commercial and I hoped "Brab" was impressed.

A curt message from Lord Brabazon's secretary that night, ordering me to attend at his office at 10 o'clock the next morning, scarcely warned of the dressing down he gave me. "Brab", who I so admired and had done so much for me, was furious! He said he was absolutely disgusted and ashamed to hear me telling a pack of lies, attempting to deceive his chairman about my interest in motor racing. He told me I was no longer a candidate for the job. He said, "You have lived and worked for motor racing because you love the sport; how dare you tell such lies!"

I completely broke down and could only stammer my apologies through my tears. What a fool I had been. What could I do? I should have known that his honesty was such that he would never behave that way himself or accept it in any other person. Directly I got home, I wrote at length, trying to apologize. For a day or two he let me sweat, then called me back to his office and said, "I think I have taught you a lesson. We will not speak of this again". Then he said, "I am on the board of David Brown Tractors and, as David Brown has just bought Aston Martin and Lagonda, I would like you to join them". This was better than I could ever have imagined, and I told him that I would be thrilled to be involved with these two firms. I had already met David Brown very briefly with Raymond Mays at Bourne and I knew his racing background with the TT Vauxhall car.

"Brab" spoke to David Brown and I was invited to the old Aston Martin works at Felton, which I knew well from my visits before the war with Jimmy Nervo. I was going to meet Claude Hill, who was developing the 2½-litre Lagonda. I had already met Claude with Jock Horsfall at the time when Jock was working on the ERA R5B "Remus". At Felton, I had a great day going through the project with Claude and driving a chassis with a couple of bucket seats, as we used to at the Bentley works at Cricklewood. I reckoned that the Lagonda would make a splendid sports/racing car for Le Mans. We understood, however, that "DB" was not too keen on the racing idea and wanted the Lagonda developed as a touring saloon.

I had an interesting meeting with David Brown himself at the new Aston Martin Lagonda showrooms in Piccadilly. He asked me if I was interested in looking after the public relations side as a consultant, as he thought it was too early to consider a full-time position in that area. I said I would be very interested indeed; he said he would discuss the matter with his sales manager and hoped that they would be able to offer me a contract within a month or two. Not exactly what I wanted, but both "Brab" and I thought that it was a good beginning.

Over tea at Eastgate House, presided over by Ann Mays, Ray once again asked me about the possibility of the ERA Club being re-formed to embrace BRM so as to promote the new car. I felt that, despite the similarity of original intentions, the BRM required a different sort of organization aimed at bringing in support from the general public, whereas the ERA Club had been

set up for motor racing enthusiasts. Ray took my point. A little later, I attended a meeting of the BRM Trust where everyone agreed that some sort of supporters' organization should be set up and I was asked if I would run it. I reckoned that this would be almost a full-time job and I was already fully employed with Peter Monkhouse at Monaco Engines; in any case, I felt it was not quite my scene. Running a supporters' club for BRM endeavours would mean working directly for the new BRM Trust, rather than for Ray and Peter and I sensed that there would be great difficulties.

Already I had seen that members of the Trust were eager to over-publicize the BRM as a potential world-beater, in contrast to Mays and Berthon who wanted to go easy on the potential until the car was proved. Another organizer for a BRM supporters' club was therefore sought, but I agreed to be on an advisory committee.

Donald Bastow with John Weatheritt's 2.5-litre Lagonda. This is the sports/racing model the author hoped the firm would produce in 1949.

PART V

BRM DAYS

Joining Alfred Owen and Raymond Mays with BRM. Our Cooper days and a serious HWM-Jaguar accident. Leaving BRM.

CHAPTER
SEVENTEEN

I saw a lot of Donald McCullough, an original member of the ERA Club who became famous as the BBC Brains Trust chairman and also as the author of best-selling books. I took Donald to Bourne because of course BRM was right up his street: immensely patriotic, he was enthusiastic about the promotion of a British Grand Prix car.

The BRM project was getting off the ground very well, with over 100 companies making parts and providing assistance. In order to co-ordinate the immense amount of work, the British Motor Racing Research Trust was formed, including the principals of some of the most important promoting companies. Among members of its committee were Alfred Owen, Chairman and Managing Director of Rubery Owen; Bernard Scott of Joseph Lucas; Tony Vandervell, Chairman of Vandervell Products; David Brown, Chairman of David Brown Tractors and Aston Martin Lagonda; Percy Bilton, Chairman of the Vigzol Oil Company; A C Burdon, Chairman of Automotive Products; and Denis Flather, Managing Director of Flather Steel in Sheffield. Donald McCullough was asked to chair the Trust. This was a very good appointment, well-suited to his skill and great sense of humour: vitally necessary because all the members of the Trust and, in fact, the senior executives of nearly all the other companies involved in the BRM project, were big and important people, used to getting their own way in running their own companies. Co-operating in a project like BRM presented many problems and Donald's infectious good humour and light touch was essential to control meetings of the Trust when so many people had their own idea of how to run a motor racing project.

My next meeting at Bourne was to advise on the organization of the supporters' club. To that end I met a member of the Trust, Percy Bilton of Vigzol Oil and one of his directors, Walter Hill. They were going to be responsible for the supporters' organization. I suggested that it should be called the BRM Association, because I thought that "supporters club" sounded too schoolboy-ish. In retrospect I think I was wrong. It should have been called the BRM Supporters' Club, because that was

Alfred G B Owen, Chairman and Joint Managing Director of Rubery, Owen and Co. in his office at Darlaston, Staffordshire, 1949.

exactly what it was; it had a very young membership, but had a wide appeal. Walter Hill had a London office and staff; he ran the organization very well indeed and it grew at a great rate.

At that same meeting with Percy Bilton I also met Alfred Owen for the first time. This was of momentous importance to me and it set the direction for the rest of my life. Alfred Owen said he knew of the surveys I had made for Lord Brabazon and the ACV group of companies. He asked if I would visit the principal companies in his group to suggest how they could be better integrated and work together to help BRM. He said Donald McCullough had recommended the idea. We talked for about 20 minutes and I knew that this was the opportunity I had been looking for, so I eagerly accepted his invitation to visit his companies and make a report.

Alfred Owen, popularly known as "AGB", was a very strong personality. Tall, dark, with an open face, he had kind but penetrating eyes and a very quiet and relaxed voice and manner. He radiated quiet confidence. He obviously knew exactly what he wanted, but his assurance was such that he spoke quietly, with great modesty and smiles. He told me that he had not followed motor racing so far, but he believed that the BRM project was important to Great Britain. He remembered that, before the war, when the Government had refused to build machines for the Schneider Trophy Air Race, Lady Houston provided the backing. The result was that the Supermarine seaplanes won the Trophy for Great Britain. This led to the development of the Rolls-Royce Merlin engine and the Spitfire fighter. So although Alfred Owen was not my sort of car enthusiast, his enthusiasm for BRM was tremendous.

Over the next week or two I visited nine or ten companies in the Midlands, the North, in Wales and in London, some with Alfred Owen and some alone. I learned a little about the Rubery Owen Group: very diverse and mostly in steel. The group's principal customers were firms in the motor, aircraft and building industries, with a very great variety of items. All the companies were wholly owned by the Owen family under the Chairman and Joint Managing Director, AGB and his younger brother Ernest. It was a completely paternalistic set-up, AGB being "the Master". In every sense this seemed to be the very best traditional sort of management. Unions and strikes were nasty things that happened to other people elsewhere! There was even a special factory called "the Sons of Rest", where employees who had passed retirement age worked at their own rate at the times when they wanted to. Everywhere I saw there was mutual respect and affection between management and workers. Of course, nobody had any rights; they did not need them. Such a situation is quite unthinkable in industry today.

However, when I talked with the senior executives of the various companies in the group I found little enthusiasm for the BRM. "Fancy the Governor getting involved with motor racing; just a way of spending money." I also found that nearly all the companies in the group were rather isolated, only interested in their own activities and not knowledgeable about the rest of the Group. The situation was absolutely ripe for public relations, so I made my report to AGB. Needless to say my report recommended that I should forthwith be appointed public relations officer of the Group.

About ten days later George Monkhouse contacted me saying that he had a promising vacancy in the Kodak company with him. This was exciting and I always got on very well with George; but Rubery Owen and BRM were even more enticing. So I telephoned AGB's office asking if he wanted to employ me. AGB was at a board meeting but sent word through his secretary saying he wanted me to join his company straight away. I turned down the Kodak job and that was how I joined Rubery Owen: no mention of salary, or any terms and conditions at all, just a telephone message that AGB wanted me to join him.

Thus I became Group Public Relations Officer of the Owen organization and remained in that position for the next 20 years, responsible only to AGB and with a small personal staff at the group's London office. I was extremely happy and (only realizing it much later) very spoiled. Alfred Owen was an extraordinary character. Firstly, he was deeply religious. At Cambridge he had studied to be an Anglican priest. At 21, when his father died suddenly, he gave up his ecclesiastical studies and took over his father's role directing Rubery Owen.

To everyone's amazement he told the staff and workers that he was going to run the company on strictly Christian lines. He really meant it and carried it through. He was a lay preacher and could be regarded as puritanical in his personal life; he was a teetotaller and non-smoker. You well might think that such a man would be intolerably prudish, narrow-minded and solemn. He was not any of those things. He was surprisingly broadminded, not expecting anyone else to lead his abstemious kind of life and was cheerful and happy in his relationships. In fact he inspired a special sort of devotion from countless employees and was more loved and respected than any other captain of industry I have known – and I have met many. He succeeded in every direction and the companies grew and prospered.

I was enthusiastic about everything about my appointment. AGB suggested a salary that was very fair although not high. He asked me if I would need any staff, telling me that I would be located in the London sales office at Market Place, Oxford Circus and there would be the usual telephone, teleprinter and typist pool facilities. I told him that I already had a good private secretary in Esme Temple and that I would like her to join me in the Owen organization. That was agreed straight away. Then he asked me about a car, telling me that he and his brother had current Bentleys and all other directors and senior executives in the group had Austin A90s. I did not want an Austin A90 and was keen to have a Jaguar. So I took a deep breath and said that, as Rubery Owen was an important supplier to Jaguar, it would be appropriate for me to have one, say a 1½-litre saloon, which would be very economical. Again, this was agreed straight away. I learned later that the rest of the group were horrified. A Jaguar and a private secretary who would travel with him! Good heavens! What on earth was the Governor thinking of? A PRO! From the world of motor racing!

CHAPTER
EIGHTEEN

During my first week at Kent House, Alfred Owen came over for some meetings and was going to see me. Typically, his meetings went on and on and at 6 o'clock, when the rest of the office was packing up, he asked me to stay behind. He said he would be eating before he caught his train home from Kings Cross and would I join him so that we could talk?

I was very pleased to and at about 6.45 pm we set off in my Jaguar. I thought we might be going to Grosvenor House, because I knew that he met Raymond Mays there. But AGB directed me to King's Cross station, where he led the way to the self-service buffet. We each collected trays and when he picked sausages and mash, a mug of tea and a couple of biscuits, I followed suit.

We had a very enjoyable meal. AGB told me the latest BRM news and arranged for me to meet the head of the Boys' Brigade, a friend of his, at Kent House the next day.

I was learning quickly. Alfred Owen was completely unspoiled and unimpressed by his own position. In the strongest and finest sense he was simple and straightforward. I drove home realizing more than ever how very lucky I was.

At the beginning, things were a little fraught because AGB appointed a public relations committee comprising six of the most powerful managing directors in the group, together with the financial director of Rubery Owen, to guide me. Since all that committee was anti-BRM I had a battle on my hands, but with AGB behind me it was an enjoyable and exciting one, which I was confident we would win.

There were 30 companies in the group but it was growing at a great rate and there were more than 100 before I left 20 years later. It was the largest group of companies in private hands in Great Britain.

Very soon after I joined the company, AGB – typically – opened two new factories in the depressed area of South Wales. There I had the great pleasure of meeting Nye Bevan and his witty wife, Jenny Lee. Tea with them in their humble cottage was followed by rides in the Jaguar. At dinner Donald McCullough and Jenny Lee sparked off one another brilliantly, to the great amusement of Nye Bevan and AGB.

Using my "Rembrandt" technique in the Rubery organisation, I started arranging group dinners for our suppliers and customers, together with our directors and sales personnel. To celebrate the 100,000th plough for Ferguson I arranged a party at Darlaston with the press. To everyone's surprise, this was a party with champagne – with AGB's agreement. This at last did me a bit of good within the Group.

Soon after I joined Rubery Owen and just when he was starting another engineering company, my great friend Peter Monkhouse was killed racing in the Mille Miglia in a Healey Silverstone. Peter was not driving himself; the co-driver was at the wheel. His wife, Peggy, was expecting their first child. There had been a good deal of tragedy in Peter's short life, but he had a dynamic personality; so much so that Peter's influence lived on very strongly with those whose lives were close to him. In a strange and sad way some could not really accept his death. This became a sad reflection on his life.

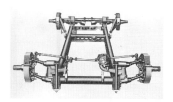

Rubery Owen chassis for the BRM V16.

British industry needed dollars, so AGB sent me off to America and Canada to visit companies in New York, Toronto, Montreal and Quebec. I was to travel first class in the *Queen Mary*. When I discussed the trip with "Pom" and Elsa Pomeroy, a rising star in musical comedy, the latter remembered that Alec Guinness and Irene Worth would be sailing on the *Queen Mary* at that time to play in *The Cocktail Party* on Broadway. Elsa therefore arranged for me to meet them on the ship. On my meeting Alec for the first time, he asked me if I had done this trip before. When he learned that it was all new to me he explained the drill. He said that those five days at sea on the Cunarder would be five days "not counting": not in England under the King, nor in America under the President, only on the *Queen Mary* under the Captain. He added, "I understand on very good authority that the Lord above does not count those five days". He said that if I was on my own, he was sure I would have a jolly good time! I took the point. He was right, but when I conveyed Alec's theory to someone I was dancing with that night, she said, "From a woman's point of view, I think there is a snag somewhere".

On RMS Queen Mary: *Bob and Mary Cummings.*

On the ship I also met Bob and Mary Cummings, the Hollywood star, so altogether we had a very enjoyable theatrical party. When I told them that I was looking forward to seeing the Manhattan Skyline as we approached New York, they said it would be far too early in the morning – about 7 o'clock. They had seen it all before, but I was determined not to miss it. As we rounded the Statue of Liberty, to my great disappointment there was a thick mist and there seemed to be nothing to see at all. Then suddenly I realized I was looking too low. High in the sky, rising out of the mist with the sun shining on it, there was what looked like a wonderful enchanted city. This view of skyscrapers glinting in the sunlight and growing up out of the clouds was one of the most moving sights I have ever seen, more beautiful and more glamorous to my mind than Rome, Paris, Venice or Baghdad.

Before going ashore, I told Bob Cummings that I wanted to

buy Penny a special present, some silk camiknickers – where should I go? Bob said, "Go to Macy's in New York. I will give you my card with a message for the manager and I am sure they will look after you well".

Right from the start, New York was very exciting. Immediately I booked in at my hotel the telephone rang and a very American voice said, "Welcome to New York, Mr Rivers Fletcher". He told me he was the president of one of the principal banks and that, while in New York, I should not use taxis because his Cadillac was outside my hotel with his chauffeur. They would be at my disposal all the time. I could not believe it. He went on to say, "What are you doing tonight?" I told him that, as I had just booked in and had never been to New York before, I had no plans at all. His reply was, "Well, you will have to eat", and he and his wife would be very honoured if I would join them as their guest for dinner that night at the Waldorf Astoria. Additionally, since I was alone, "would I like a companion? Which would I prefer – a blonde or a brunette?" I honestly cannot remember what I said, but I know I had a good time. It was like that wherever I went in America and Canada. This was something quite new to me and of course was not really for me at all. The fact was that it had been well publicized in the American press that a representative of Alfred Owen, Chairman and Managing Director of one of the leading groups of companies in Great Britain, was visiting. All the principal banks vied with one another to look after me in the hope that, if and when the Owen organization enlarged its scope in America and Canada, their banks would be concerned.

The next day I went to Macy's big store, a sort of New York version of Selfridges or Harrods. I produced Bob Cummings' card and there was no doubt about the effect: the manager appeared himself and handed me over to a charming girl assistant to learn my requirements.

I told her that I wanted some pairs of silk camiknickers for my wife. She looked blank and said, "What are they? I have never heard of them". I explained and drew a picture. "Oh, teddies!" she said. Apparently, that is what they are called in America. I was then immediately able to buy some. I asked the assistant why they were called "teddies". She told me that when Edward Prince of Wales visited New York, he always bought these items for his girlfriends and so they became known as "teddies". I understand they are fashionable again in Britain, still called "teddies", but I guess few people know the origin.

My return trip, again on the *Queen Mary*, was also a memorable one because we encountered one of the biggest Atlantic storms ever. The *Queen Mary* – of course this was long before stabilizers appeared – rolled to a greater degree than ever before or since. I am very fortunate in that I am seldom seasick and I confess I enjoyed every moment of the excitement. Strapping myself to the rails, I was able to take some fine photographs. Inevitably, quite a few people were injured; there were a number of broken limbs, but nothing very serious. At the height of the storm a grand piano got away from its moorings and went right through a bulkhead. That was the worst of the damage to the ship, but of course the breakage of crockery reached astronomical levels. Yet after the storm there were always enough cups and plates. Such wonderful organization!

On the ship I met the American cast of "Call me Madam". One of the stars, Marion Ross, invited me to their first night in London. She and two more of the cast were going to have dinner with Penny and me after the show.

Due to the storm, we were very late at Southampton. We berthed at about 11.00 pm, but no disembarkation could take place until the next morning. I knew that Penny was meeting the ship. I thought that she would have to go back to her hotel that night and meet me the next morning, but we had an amazing bit of luck.

I had spent so much time on the ship with the cast of "Call Me Madam" and the star, Marion Ross, that they were anxious to meet Penny. They therefore persuaded the captain to bring her on to the ship that night. When the *Queen Mary* berthed, the captain was the only person who went ashore and he had Penny paged. Sitting at a late dinner at the captain's table with Marion Ross, I was amazed to see Penny coming into the dining room on the arm of the captain.

Above left:
Atlantic photographed from the Queen Mary.

Above right:
The great storm: another view.

This was all out of order, of course, but Penny joined us for dinner, stayed the night in my cabin and breakfasted with all the cast of "Call Me Madam" the next morning before we disembarked. Penny had to be personally escorted ashore because she had not been a passenger and had no passport or other documentation, so only the captain was able to get her through Customs.

Over the next 20 years I had many trips to and from the States on the *Queen Mary* and the *Queen Elizabeth*, all before stabilizers and sometimes encountering heavy seas, but nothing like that first storm.

On one occasion I sailed with Eddie Hall and our long talks on the Derby Bentley led me to acquire a near-replica some years later. Eddie was on his way to see a musical on Broadway, show business being his second interest after motor racing. On his suggestion to the Captain of the *Queen Mary*, I put on a show of my motor racing films to some of the crew and passengers. This became a regular feature of my trips on the old Cunarders during the 1950s.

Saturday, 26 August 1950 was the start of the *Daily Express* International Trophy at Silverstone. Raymond Sommer at the wheel of the BRM V16 failed to start in its first race, when both driving shafts broke. That story has been told a million times. The failure in itself was not significant, but its timing and the devastating publicity was such that I do not believe that BRM or Raymond Mays ever quite recovered from the occasion. Neither the eventual great success of the marque, nor the later accolades, ever eradicated the disappointment of that day. Unfair and unjustified adverse publicity and public relations have a lot to answer for.

Above left:
With Marion Ross on the Queen Mary.

Above right:
At the caravan: John Winter, Johnnie Morgan and Roy Nockolds with Esme and Penny.

Below:
First BRM V16 engine.

Raymond Mays driving the first BRM V16; a demonstration for the Press at Folkingham.

After my first 1½-litre Jaguar, my next Owen organization car was one of my favourites. AGB suggested that I should have a Mark VII Jaguar, but he allowed me to have instead a rather special Mark V, because I preferred that model as it was nimbler. My Mark V came by way of the Jaguar Competition Department, through "Lofty" England. One of the last Mark Vs produced, it had steel connecting rods and Mark VII handbrake among the modifications. The styling department at Jaguar liked my special rear wing spats. The stylists would have standardized these if that model had been continued.

My Mark V was an easy 100 mph car, its only fault being the poor brakes. This was just before the use of disc brakes became general and, at that time, nearly all large fast cars were similarly lacking in this area.

At last on 30 September 1950 at Goodwood we had a really good day with BRM. Despite appalling conditions, Reg Parnell won both of his races in the V16. In the big race, the Goodwood Trophy, with the rain falling heavily, I thought Reg would never be able to contend with "Bira" and de Graffenried in their Maseratis. Although the BRM had a lot more power and was faster in a straight line, the Maseratis were fully developed cars with excellent roadholding. Additionally, both "Bira" and de Graffenried had already had a lot of experience with their machines.

Everything was against the BRM; neither the brakes nor the steering were quite right and Reg had very little experience with the car at all – only one very short drive in the rain at Folkingham, when the brakes were playing up. Yet he drove

Above left:
Barcelona: Peter Berthon, Donald McCullough, Peter Walker, Ken Richardson, David Brown and Walter Hill.

Above right:
Silverstone: at the BRMA tent – Esme with my Mark V Jaguar and her Austin Seven.

magnificently: right on the limit all the way, never putting a foot wrong. I consider that this was one of Reg Parnell's best drives, at the time when he was absolutely at the zenith of his driving career. His win was of the utmost importance for the BRM, in fact almost vital to the continuation of the project after the débacle at Silverstone.

Although Barcelona was a failure, it did the team good to see that the BRM was the fastest car on the straight, against all the Continentals. It was clear that we had the power and the drivers to apply it on a straight road. So it looked to me as though we were nearly there. Only a little more roadholding and some reliability and we would be real competitors in Grands Prix. That is what we thought and hoped – and hoped!

Throughout 1950, BRM staggered from crisis to crisis, never finding the required reliability, nor enough roadholding. Publicity and public relations for BRM was handled by Donald McCullough and I was only concerned with the Rubery Owen end of it. Poor Donald had an impossible task: costs were rising all the time and finance was running out. Our suppliers were getting fed up without any Grand Prix victories. It is too easy to say that too much was promised too early. Of course that was so, but the BRM could only get the support needed if it could be shown that it had the potential to win. It was simply impractical to play down the project.

If, say, Rolls-Royce, Mercedes-Benz or General Motors had set out to do what BRM tried to do, they would have gone about it quite differently. They would have been able to tackle the project on the right kind of scale, designing and building many experimental prototypes, probably crashing some, taking the necessary time for everything, having withall the continuous backing of a large motor manufacturing business. They would not have needed to shout the odds, or indeed claim anything at all, until the cars were ready for winning.

BRM needed the publicity to keep going at all, so Donald McCullough had to try everything to persuade the backers to continue their support. With skill and a great deal of good humour, he performed a difficult task as well as it could have been done; it was not at all an enviable job.

At a time when nearly the whole British press was damning the BRM as a ridiculously complicated design taking far too long to make and the organization for making all the wrong decisions, we had a welcome visit from Alfred Neubauer, the Mercedes team manager. He was full of praise for the design and was amazed that so much progress had been made with such a minute organization. He told us that it would have taken Mercedes nearly as long, even with their hundreds of men working on the project. It was comforting to hear his praise, but he feared that our aims were hopelessly beyond our limited resources.

Having travelled with us to racing events for a year or two, "Beano" Ibbotson and my secretary Esme married. In the fullness of time they had a daughter, Sally, and Penny and I were her godparents. It was all very nice indeed, but I had to look for another private secretary. After interviewing many, Brenda Bowman appeared – too young and, I thought, too pretty for peace of mind. However, her driving experience had been in her father's Mark V Jaguar, exactly like mine and she was cheerfully enthusiastic about the job. So for all the wrong reasons she became my private secretary.

Goodwood: the BRM all ready for Reg Parnell.

In fact, it was a splendid choice. The job was expanding all the time, but Brenda coped very well and we enjoyed one another's company. Together we covered a lot of promising but disappointing BRM races. At Turnberry in Scotland, however, we were able to record another victory by Reg Parnell.

In those relatively carefree days, we were able to walk all round the circuits on the very edge of the track, sit filming on the straw bales defining the corners and even cross the track to film on the other side while the races were in progress. John Eason-Gibson, later secretary of the British Racing Drivers' Club, was a special help to us, claiming – quite rightly – that officially accepted photographers should be allowed to use their own discretion and not be restricted by rules and regulations.

CHAPTER NINETEEN

The Bugatti Type 35 high on the banking at Great Auclum, 1951.

I was very happy with my road motoring in new Jaguars to my specification from the Owen Organisation. I was very spoiled by Alfred Owen. So for racing I did not want a sports car. The only road car that I would have liked was a 4½-litre Invicta. My couple of years with one of those low chassis Invictas when I was with Raymond Mays and Peter Berthon in the 1930s left me with a strong love for that model.

The chassis and a few parts of the prototype 5-litre supercharged Invicta which Raymond Mays was hoping to build was still around, and I hoped that one day we could do something about it. Donald Monro, whom I got to know in 1929 when he was competing with a special 18/80 MG, had become very Invicta-minded. Firstly, with 3-litre and then with 4½-litre chassis models. I had some good drives with Donald with his very short chassis model called "Red Gauntlet". We were both interested in altering the bodies of our cars to our designs, forever comparing drawings and making changes. Now I was considering a sports Invicta for myself, but finally decided to buy a Grand Prix racing car.

As I had seen a lot of good Bugatti racing at Brooklands before the war and driven most of the best models, including our Club Type 51, I just had to have a Grand Prix Bugatti of my own. As a result of my experience with Earl Howe, my real longing was for a Type 59, but this model was way beyond my purse. I would have liked a supercharged Type 35 or 51, but again they were too expensive. I also saw a couple of Type 37s, which I had known and driven before the war. However, when Jack Bartlett showed me the unblown straight-eight Type 35 that I was familiar with when Kay Petre raced it, I fell for that car straight away.

Jack was a good friend whom I had known for many years. At his premises in West London, he always had a good selection of the right sort of cars.

Another old friend, Stafford-East, one of the best Bugatti

engineers, checked it over for me and very generously taught two young friends of mine how to maintain the car. My young mechanics were David Yiend, a rabid (actually too rabid!) enthusiast and his close friend, Tony Hitchcock, a dental student at Guy's Hospital. They were both in their late teens, members of the North London Enthusiasts' Car Club and lived at Hemel Hempstead.

With my ex-Marcus Chambers Riley Nine Monaco saloon as tow car, and the Bugatti on a fixed tow bar, David and Tony brought the Bugatti to all our events. Penny and I drove the Mark V Jaguar and for three years we ran the Bugatti in nearly every possible race and hillclimb.

To own and race a Grand Prix Bugatti is tremendously rewarding. This was one of the most important and enjoyable experiences in my life.

At Prescott I made the fastest unsupercharged Bugatti time on the hill and held that record for some years. Our young mechanics did a great job and became almost part of the family. When Tony qualified as a dentist I became one of his patients. His work was equally meticulous on the car and on the person.

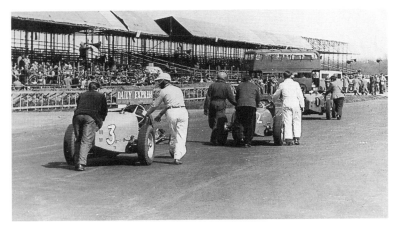 

Above right:
Prescott 1951: winning the Bugatti Handicap, and breaking the record for unsupercharged Bugattis.

Above left:
Tony Hitchcock and the author push the Type 35 on to the grid at Silverstone. The other Bugattis are Blomfield's Type 37 and Baron's Type 51. Guy Griffiths.

David Yiend was an extraordinary young man whose enthusiasm for motor racing overcame everything else, even his good sense. On one occasion when we were going to Shelsley Walsh, Penny and I left early in the Jaguar to meet some friends. Tony and Brenda drove the Riley, with David on tow behind in the Bugatti. They stopped out in the country for a picnic lunch. David said he just wanted to check something on the Bugatti's engine. So they took the tow bar off and gave David just a push to start the engine – nothing more than that.

As soon as it fired David accelerated away into the distance, out of sight. Tony and Brenda were horrified. Instead of reappearing in a few moments which would have been bad enough, David was away for about half an hour while Tony and Brenda remained with the Riley in a terrible panic. The racing Bugatti, unlicensed, uninsured and unsilenced, a Grand Prix car, was being driven by a fanatical and comparatively inexperienced teenage enthusiast!

On his eventual return David said he just could not help it. The temptation was irresistible. He just had to drive that racing Bugatti as fast as he could. By good fortune he did not have an accident and did not even come across the police although he said that he drove as hard as he could all the time.

That was David. He begged Tony and Brenda not to tell me and they did not until later, after his death. Poor David: he never could contain his enthusiasm. Some time later he was killed on the road, driving his own Riley Nine saloon; fortunately no one else was involved. He had to race, he just could not wait. I am sure he would have become a racing driver if he had lived. Whether or not he would have been successful we will never know, but he would have needed a lot of luck to have survived that period when his enthusiasm outstripped his reason.

Contrasting air-cooled racing cars, both very successful in the hillclimbs. Colin Strang with his 500 and Sydney Allard with his Steyr-Allard.

For a time I was responsible for the Bugatti Owners' Club annual dinner and dance, which Brenda and I put on at the Dorchester. One year we staged a novel cabaret. After the dinner all the lights were dimmed, a record played the noise of a Bugatti being revved up. Spotlights were trained on the double doors and my young seven-year-old son, Peter, in appropriate racing garb, drove in at speed in a miniature Type 52 Bugatti and did two laps of the dance floor, pulling up in front of the band. It was great fun and the timing was spot on: thanks to a couple of practice runs in the afternoon, when Peter overdid the cornering, slid off the dance floor into the kitchen and nearly wrote off a large trolley of glasses.

Having married off Esme to my oldest friend, "Beano", we saw the same thing happening with Brenda and Tony Hitchcock. Their marriage was a very swish affair at the Savoy Chapel, with a large reception at the Savoy Hotel. My younger son, Jeremy, was their page in full Scottish dress. He was wearing the Royal Stuart tartan, although our family claim to it is extremely dubious, based on a poorly substantiated ancestral royal liaison, on the wrong side of the duvet!

Jeremy did a roaring trade for himself collecting coins from all the guests in his sporran, encouraged by Brenda's father, who suggested that he was saving up for his own Bugatti.

With far too many BRM failures and with most members of the Trust losing faith in the project, the whole outfit was put up for sale late in 1952. Not surprisingly the only really serious bidder was Sir Alfred Owen, steadfast as ever. When he told me that his offer was being accepted and BRM would be ours, I was highly delighted.

The fact that BRM was being sold was going to be announced by Donald McCullough on behalf of the Trust. This was to take place at a press meeting to be convened at the Royal Thames Yacht Club in London.

Although it was generally hoped and believed by now that Alfred Owen would buy BRM, the Trust agreed that the disclosure should be made only by the purchaser. Just before the press meeting AGB told me that, because Basil Cardew, Motoring Editor of the *Daily Express*, had been very fair to him and BRM during the last year or so, he had promised him that he would give that paper the exclusive story that Alfred Owen was the purchaser of BRM.

Peter with the miniature Type 53 Bugatti at the Dorchester.

I was astonished and horrified. I realized that this was an impossible situation, so I told AGB that he could not do that. I explained that all the media people were going to be present to learn who the purchaser was and that we, Rubery Owen, needed to tell them all – not just one newspaper. I explained that if I obeyed his instructions I would have to say nothing at all to anyone and just let the *Daily Express* publish the story next morning. All the Press would be furious, and would damn us quite rightly. AGB said he had given his promise and he was bound to keep it. So I said, "Right, you stick to your promise but I will not obey you. I'll tell the whole story to everyone. Basil Cardew will be furious, but what can he do? He is no fool; he knows very well what I have got to do. We may just lose the support of the *Express* for a time, but that would be much better than losing all credibility with the Press for ages".

Reluctantly, AGB agreed with me and that is what happened. Basil Cardew was absolutely furious with me. "Alfred Owen will have to sack you", is what he said – to AGB, with me standing beside him. AGB said he was sorry, and then put on that blank look that he was rather good at.

I must admit I was rather worried, but that night when AGB said good night to me he was smiling. Basil Cardew was, and still is, a big man and when I saw him two or three days later he put his arm round me and said, "You are a swine" – and then he laughed and said, "Come on, let's have lunch". He said that, if it had not been for me, he would have got away with it, but he knew that it would have been an absurd situation. We have been good friends ever since.

From now on, BRM publicity was mine, but oh what a problem it was! My brief from AGB was quite simple: make sure that the Owen organization gets good publicity from BRM. However, the BRM was a music hall joke; we did not win any Grands Prix. The background to the purchase of the racing car project was only failure.

None of our managing directors was pleased that we now owned the BRM and it was generally believed that I had been a very bad influence on the Chairman in the whole matter. I certainly had supported him as far as I could, but Alfred Owen was always very much his own man and I do not think anyone could have influenced him much in one way or another. In support of BRM he was as steadfast as ever.

With BRM part of the Owen organization, the BRMA club wanted to go on supporting the cars, so AGB provided the group with an office and facilities at Kent House, asking me to give every sort of assistance.

BRMA changed its name to Owen Racing Motor Association and the manager, Fred Tinto, moved into an office next to mine. Brenda's assistant, Betty Gabb-Jones, was seconded to ORMA for secretarial duties and the arrangements went well. The membership started to grow again with greater future security promised within the Owen organization.

My next private secretary was Isobel Robinson. I would like to have said that I met her and forthwith engaged her. In fact it did not happen that way at all. While I was away in America, Fred Tinto advertised for a junior typist for ORMA and Isobel took that job. When I came back to England she was installed in the next office with Tinto and Betty Gabb-Jones, Brenda's assistant.

Isobel, very attractive with light auburn hair, was only 20. She was already quite knowledgeable about cars and motor racing because she knew Eric Giles, the secretary of the Bugatti Owners' Club and his family in the Woking – Guildford area, where they all lived.

With Brenda devoting more of her time and attention to Tony Hitchcock, I borrowed Isobel for a lot of my work, particularly the jobs away in other parts of the country. She took to the work and when Brenda left for her married role, Isobel became my private secretary. It is difficult to describe someone with whom I worked closely for 10 years and who has been one of my closest friends for more than 35. Isobel's own assessment of our working relationship is that I was an ideas man while she did the detailed work and I suppose that is about right.

She straight away joined our family team in motor racing events, as well as with BRM and developed a straight-arm driving position at the wheel of my Jaguar. Isobel soon bought an MG Y-type 1250 cc saloon, which she drove in practice at Prescott before competing with her early Broadley Special. Not the least discouraged by a lot of mechanical disasters that would have put off anyone less enthusiastic, she struggled on with the Broadley Special until she replaced it with a delightful BMC-engined Turner, which she bought from Betty Haig. With that Turner Isobel was extremely successful in all the sprints and hillclimbs: she was one of the fastest lady drivers.

Isobel in the Turner at Prescott. Charles Dunn.

For BRM hopes, Albi in 1953 had to be the great possibility. On test the cars were now going splendidly. Our team was going to be Juan Manuel Fangio, Froilan Gonzalez and Ken Wharton and it could not have been a stronger one. Last-minute entries of Alberto Ascari in a works Ferrari and Giuseppe Farina in Tony Vandervell's Thinwall provided the right opposition.

I asked AGB if I could take Penny with me to France to help with the filming. This was agreed and we had a most enjoyable four days filming Toulouse-Lautrec's famous city, all the practice and the racing. We had no mechanical troubles in practice, Fangio just pipped Ascari for the fastest lap and pole position at the last minute as practice was flagged off. The only worry was Gonzalez throwing a nearside rear tyre tread, damaging the

The nearside rear treads that spoiled our Albi effort: Fangio's stop in the final.

exhaust pipe. On a very fast right-handed circuit all the BRMs showed excessive wear on the nearside rear tyres. When it was suggested that the exhausts blowing out close to the rear tyres might be overheating them, Vic Barlow of Dunlop checked the temperature of all the tyres. He found that the inside rear tyres were only normally warm, establishing that it was not the exhaust layout that caused the excessive heat, but the wear.

On the day, amid terrific excitement, Fangio won his heat and easily secured the lap record. The start of the final was sensational. Ascari was between Fangio and Gonzalez on the front row. Ray and I positioned ourselves at the exit of the first corner immediately beyond the pits; Ray with his stopwatch while I was poised with my movie camera. In the pits Penny and Lorna Berthon kept a second lap chart.

When the cars were starting the noise was stupendous. Sensing the tension Charles Faroux, the official starter, dropped the flag early and Fangio just led Ascari as the pack streamed off.

The racing that day was the most exciting I have ever seen, with the big powerful cars driven to their limits. Fangio continued to lead with Ascari snapping at his heels until the Ferrari blew up, soon followed by Farina in the Thinwall: the Ferrari engines were unable to match the speed of the BRM.

For a time we were lying first, second and third, our dreams coming true. However, disaster struck as all the BRMs threw those nearside treads; Fangio's caused serious trouble, which forced him to retire. Then Ken Wharton had the most terrible-looking accident, losing the car at about 150 mph, turning end over end. Ken was thrown out, but miraculously unhurt; the car

Fangio at speed winning his heat.

was written off completely. Gonzalez still led the field until a second tyre disaster lost him so much time that he was only able to finish second to Louis Rosier.

Although we only won the heat, Albi will always be remembered as the V16's greatest race – a tribute to the design of the BRM and the courage of the drivers.

Those great days of the BRM V16 and Tony Vandervell's Thinwall are unforgettable, as are the star drivers and personalities of that period, the like of which we will never see again in Grand Prix racing. Quite rightly I was never given the opportunity of driving a BRM in a race. It was only through the generosity of Raymond Mays and Sir Alfred that I was allowed to sample the V16 Mark II and the later P25 on test.

As I am often asked what driving the V16 was like, I try to describe it in this way:

Far left:
Fangio tries the V16 BRM at Silverstone: Froilan Gonzalez, Raymond Mays, Eric Greene, Peter Berthon and Ken Wharton. G Monkhouse.

Left:
Lorna Berthon with Fangio.

Driving an ordinary A or B-type 1½-litre ERA on a long straight, you put your foot down on the loud pedal and the car goes up to about 130 mph. You do have to concentrate a bit, keeping it straight, but it is all quite straightforward. Driving the V16 BRM you start it in the same way, but you get 130 mph at half-throttle. When you press the loud pedal right down, you suddenly get wheelspin, both rear wheels produce smoke. You are very busy trying to keep the car straight and, if it is me driving, the foot comes off the loud pedal very smartly.

Below far right:
Tony Vandervell and Pete Collins in the 4½-litre Thinwall-Ferrari, with Alfred Owen.

Below:
The remains after Ken Wharton's accident.

Right/far right:
Gonzalez collects a stake as he runs out of road at Silverstone. Removed by a marshal.

Peter Berthon watches while Tony Vandervell plugs in the electric starter to the Tipo 125 Thinwall-Ferrari.
G Monkhouse.

Now, I like wheelspin, which is great fun in a simple sports car on a roundabout in the wet. I can manage that, but not at 130 mph in the dry in a BRM. That is only for the real racing drivers!

My Cooper days were my salad days; everything during that period from about 1953 until 1959, is etched on my memory. It all came right – just luck. I suppose there is a time for all of us when we are on the top of our form, such as it is. In respect of the cars it was John Cooper who gave me the chance: "500" tests at Goodwood; and Prescott. Then a little later, there was another test at Goodwood in an 1100 with Nancy Mitchell and Stirling Moss.

Stirling and I shared an 1100 at Prescott and I was not too far behind him, so I decided to sell my Bugatti and buy a Cooper for myself. I bought from John Barber his well-used 1100 cc

Left:
See how close they were to the wheel! John Cooper at Prescott.

Below far left:
Peter Walker and Reg Parnell on the back of the grid at Silverstone.

Below:
High on the banking at Great Auclum.

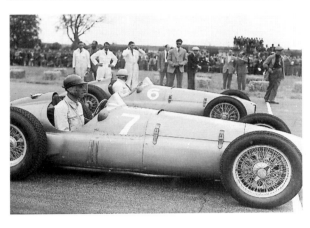

Cooper-JAP. Those were the days! I never got near the hillclimb championship, but I had a good try. We ran in as many hillclimbs as possible. However, I missed rather a lot of them because my job with BRM took precedence and many hillclimbs clashed with Grands Prix. That Series Five Cooper gave us 15 ftds and 8 course records. That sounds quite impressive, but in fact in nearly all the important national events I was beaten by the champions, Ken Wharton, Tony Marsh and David Boshier-Jones.

In 1957 I changed the car for a similar Mark VIII, which was supercharged. Freddie Owen, who was in charge of all the preparation of my Coopers, removed the blower from the Mark VIII because he feared it would be unreliable. He was proved right because, in nearly every instance, the unblown 1100s were more successful than the supercharged machines. My Mark VIII was really super, definitely faster, with better handling than the earlier car and we had nearly as many successes. Again, however, the champion drivers more often than not beat me quite easily; and a new young driver, David Good, despite the handicap of having one very short arm, usually made a better time than me.

Donald Monro continued with his Invicta racing but bought another car which I knew well before the war – the Skinner Special which Carl Skinner built. That lovely little close-coupled coupé with its big Hudson engine was tremendous fun and Donald ran it in several events. He also got very enthusiastic

Tazio Nuvolari watching practice at Silverstone.

Right:
Silverstone: Leslie Johnson in the ERA E-type with John Eason-Gibson.

Far right:
Silverstone: Zora Arkus-Duntov, Alberto Ascari and Luigi Villoresi.

about Alvis, two 12/70s and a TA 14 for which he designed a special body which was made by Jarvis at Wimbledon.

Donald was a great character. He had a thriving fruit, flower and vegetable business in Covent Garden. Starting his days very early in the morning, he often met his motor racing friends hosting enormous breakfasts in his big office at Covent Garden at about midday. His very young teenage daughter Shirley, adopted as a baby when he and his wife were in their late forties, often came to the racing events. She developed a love for the vintage scene, but circumstances prevented her from taking part for many years.

As well as driving in all the available races and hillclimbs, I decided to do some rallying, joining friends like Peter Clark and Goff Imhof in rallies organised by the NLECC of which I was the President. I drove my Mark II Jaguar and my co-drivers were my wife, Penny and Peggy Monkhouse.

I had no success at all. My navigation was hopeless; the

At last, FTD at Prescott, 1955, in the Mark V Cooper.

popular legend that I drove everywhere via Wapping Old Stairs in East London is not true, but I admit that I usually got lost.

Since I was not very good at it, I usually managed to hit the maximum number of bollards and failed to reverse into the required bays in the driving tests in those rallies – not my scene.

Far left:
Louis Chiron makes a point to Sammy Davis.

Left:
Christmas Card.

Below:
The Mark II BRMs at Goodwood, 1954: Flockhart and Wharton leaving the line in front of Pete Collins in the Thinwall-Ferrari.

CHAPTER TWENTY

Filming on the Continent, particularly at Spa and Monaco, gave us some great times. Our expenses were minimal in comparison with other public relations and film units. The situation was helped because we seldom stayed at the big hotels and we did not drink alcohol. This was nothing to do with AGB's views, only our own likes and dislikes. In fact he asked me if I would sign the pledge as he had done. "You don't like alcohol," he said, "so why not sign the pledge and set an example." I could not do that and we agreed to differ.

For the filming, we each used Kodak Royals with 16 mm magazine loading. We usually carried half a dozen extra magazines, just as George Monkhouse taught me.

I usually filmed the start, finish, pits and nearby corners, while Isobel went out into the country filming the rest of the circuit. In this way she covered the fastest and most dangerous stretches, which suited her excellent technique and courage. I was better able to get close to the action at the start and in the pits. We seldom saw one another during a Grand Prix, but we shared our anxiety till Kodak returned our processed material. Cutting, editing, writing the commentary and doing the narration was time-consuming but interesting work, which we both enjoyed.

Year after year we longed in vain to record BRM Grand Prix victories, but we made the most of every small achievement and highlighted promising future developments. For my BRM film shows I usually added a short of our amateur hillclimbs, which went down well because it was grass-roots and lighthearted.

Filming the practice for a Continental Grand Prix was important and it was essential to cover each race. We shared the excitement with John Tate, who also filmed, the regular photographers, journalists and commentators such as Gregor Grant, John Bolster, Raymond Baxter, Philip Turner, Peter Garnier, Ted Eves, Jabby Crombac, Denis Jenkinson and others. Parties after GP practice were always fun, with relaxation and much laughter with Harry Schell, Roy Salvadori, John Cooper, Stirling Moss, Mike Hawthorn, Pete Collins and the rest of the "Circus". On the circuits we were all Ferodo customers in that we enjoyed the English tea brewed up by Syd Henson, the popular Ferodo competition manager. Early on race day we usually joined Vic Barlow, Dunlop's technical representative, for breakfast. If AGB turned up for practice, which he liked to do, I had to be ready to drive him to the airport to catch his plane to England on Saturday evening so that he could preach in church on Sunday.

Perhaps it was no wonder that the staff of Rubery Owen at Darlaston used to say, "Our PRO just swans around enjoying himself motor racing". I could not help this, could I? AGB could not attend motor races on the Sabbath and as nearly all Continental Grands Prix took place on Sunday I had to represent him as the entrant of BRM.

Sometimes Penny wished to come with me to her favourite venues: Monte Carlo and Reims. AGB always agreed to this and she was a splendid assistant. On one occasion we even took our boys with us to Reims.

Basil Putt was one of several BRM team managers; Bertie Bradnack was another – it was a difficult job and it did not really work out. In the early days, Peter Berthon and Raymond Mays ran the team as they had done with Humphrey Cook

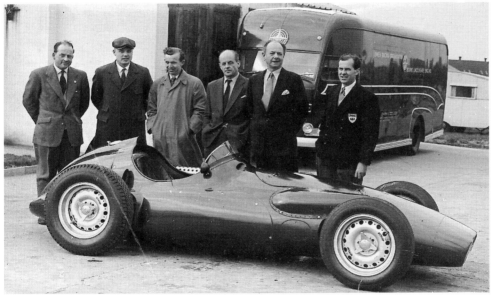

At Folkingham, 1955; the new team manager, Basil Putt, and Mike Hawthorn, Tony Brooks, Peter Berthon, Raymond Mays and the author.

before the war with ERA. The motor sport scene was now so different and the relaxed amateur administration that we had enjoyed was no longer applicable. This managerial problem was never resolved until 1962, when Tony Rudd took on the job.

Because one of the Owen Group, Motor Panels of Coventry, built the body shell, I had an Armstrong-Siddeley Sapphire, which Tommy Sopwith uprated considerably. The special high-geared steering was great on the open road, but it made the Sapphire a very heavy pig in London.

One other car that was surprisingly good, with nice handling but not much performance, was the 3-litre Austin Vanden Plas saloon. I loved an uprated and stiffened Mark X Jaguar, which I drove to and from Le Mans and round the circuit; but I never really took to my S-type Jaguar, which seemed to be rather

Folkingham, 1957, with the ORMA: Elliot Russell, Philip Shenton, Ron Flockhart, Olive Beaumont, Molly Wheeler (secretary of the ORMA), Tony Rudd, Raymond Mays, Peter Berthon and the author.

cumbersome after a Mark II. The Mark II was the Jaguar I kept longest, although from the purist point of view, I no doubt spoiled its front end - but I rather liked it.

I have enjoyed a lot of good AC motoring. I drove Ken Rudd's prototype AC Aceca and considered this car's handling to be better than any other in the same class. In fact, it was not until many years later that I came across cars whose handling gave me the same pleasure. These were Mike Spence's Lotus-BRM Elan, which I had for a time and raced at Prescott; and a Matra Coupé which I had when we were racing the BRM Matra at Le Mans.

Appreciation of handling goes somewhat beyond the purely technical science of roadholding. It is largely a personal thing, niceties of feel as subtle as the differences between the feel and touch of people's hands.

When my second son Jeremy appeared, I looked for a proper-sized family home. I had always hoped that one day I would be able to live in my grandfather's house, Lynwood, where I had spent my earliest days. However, by the 1950s the world had changed; our old house at Totteridge required a large staff, two gardeners and a lifestyle not within my grasp. This was a pity, but I could not consider Lynwood, despite the fact that the new occupant, the Lord Mayor of London, Sir Frank Newsome-Smith and his family, were good friends and were keen to sell.

However, Penny found a Victorian house at Arkley just north of Barnet and in the grounds there was a fine old barn big

enough to take about six cars – that clinched it. We changed the
name to Salhouse, a favourite Norfolk Broad. A couple of years
later we added a wing for my mother-in-law and grandmother-in-
law. Four generations altogether – well, very near and, believe it
or not, it worked like a charm. Most of the credit was due to
Penny because I was away motor racing so much.

Within the garden there were good roads right round the house
and down to the old barn, so the children would be able to learn
to drive at home before they were old enough to drive on the
road. Our neighbour was Norman Wisdom, who was mad about
cars, too, so we had a lot of fun with him, a good fast driver.
He fooled in our films.

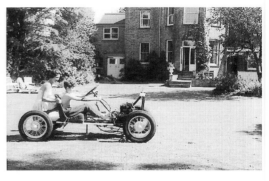

Above right:
**Jeremy's single-seater
Austin, with Penny as riding
mechanic.**

Above left:
**Peter Berthon, Raymond
Mays, the author, Jean
Behra, Harry Schell
and Tony Rudd.**

Left:
**Norman Wisdom, Rivers
Fletcher and son (Cooper)**

For the 1958 Moroccan Grand Prix at Casablanca I shared a
hired car with Stuart Lewis-Evans who was driving for Vanwall.
In the race poor Stuart had a terrible accident and was so badly
burned that he died a few days later: a death I felt very deeply,
as we had become good friends and planned to see more of one
another.

Lack of success with the P25 BRM was a continuing problem.
Isobel and I travelled all over the Continent filming each Grand

Prix, hoping that the resulting film would enhance our company's products. On some occasions this was quite impossible so at the quarterly meetings of the Owen organization managing directors my activities were often strongly criticized.

AGB's strict honesty prevented him from excusing the BRM failures and he made no attempt to prevent his co-directors speaking out against the project within the Group. Time after time he listened to their views and said quietly, "I have faith in the eventual success of BRM". He was the boss and his tremendous success in other fields was obvious, so we ploughed on.

I do not like to admit it now, but in the mid-1950s I really despaired of achieving the right results from the Bourne administration. The pressures in international motor racing were so much greater than we had been used to in the 1930s with the ERA. Now even our location at Bourne in Lincolnshire seemed to be against us. Our rivals meeting in London seemed to have a much better and closer relationship with officialdom and the Press.

I became very friendly with John Cooper and the Cooper Car Company at Surbiton. Everything about the Cooper establishment was the reverse of ours at BRM, just as John's engineering was the reverse of Peter Berthon's. It is not quite true to say that John Cooper drew his chassis in chalk on the garage floor, or that he picked up his main components from the local scrapyard. Nor is it true that every nut and bolt on the BRM had to be made to a one-off specification. Nevertheless there was that sort of difference in the respective attitudes.

As the Cooper Company grew and prospered, it soon became under-financed. John came to me and asked if there was any possibility of Alfred Owen financing Cooper and possibly organizing a closer relationship with BRM. I liked this idea and considered that somehow or other a combination of BRM and Cooper might be a proposition, so I arranged a meeting between

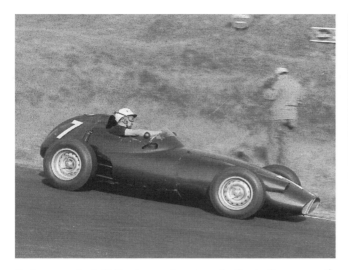

John and AGB. I understand that the meeting went well and AGB certainly liked John. However, he handed the project for assessment to our company secretary, James Glover.

After several weeks of no comment I asked Jimmy Glover how things were progressing. He gave me a funny sort of look and told me that there were many other, more important matters on his desk and the Cooper project would have to wait its turn. I raised the matter again several times and even dared to question AGB. Although the proposal was never turned down, the fact of the matter was that it was never really considered. I suppose BRM and Cooper would have been impossible bedfellows. John rang me once or twice, but the whole thing died a natural death.

We seemed to be having continual trouble with the single-disc brake of the BRM. I begged Peter Berthon to fit two normal discs on the rear wheels instead, but he and Tresilian were convinced that their unconventional three-disc system was right.

The 2½-litre engine, when they had lightened the original very large single-inlet valve, was proving reliable and was giving at

Above left:
Joakim Bonnier wins the Dutch Grand Prix, 1959.

Above right:
Joakim Bonnier, Peter Berthon, Jean Behra, Sir Alfred Owen and Raymond Mays.

The chassis for the Cooper-BRM, with Rob Walker and Alf Francis.

Brenda Bowman and Joan Gerard at Goodwood.

least as much horsepower as any of the opposition. I thought it would prove to be a winner in a little rear-engined Cooper chassis. I discussed this with Rob Walker, suggesting to him that he should fit a BRM engine in a Cooper for Stirling Moss to drive. Stirling was keen on the idea and when I suggested it to AGB he was in favour. With lukewarm approval from Bourne, a BRM engine was loaned to Rob Walker. The engine was installed in one of the Walker-Cooper chassis by Alf Francis.

After a very brief trial Stirling raced it at Aintree but had transmission trouble. He tried it again at Monaco, but there was still more trouble with the transmission. Stirling in the Cooper-BRM was in fact faster than anyone in a Cooper-Climax, but this was by dint of his driving ability: he himself was faster still in a Cooper-Climax. The BRM engine was therefore returned to Bourne and that finally was the end of the Cooper-BRM project. Alf Francis claimed that the BRM engine gave less power than the units in the works cars and, in any case, it was agreed that more development would have been required to make the Cooper-BRM project viable.

At that time Stirling Moss was much faster than any other driver. He was, however, having difficulty in deciding what car to drive. Some wrong decisions were made with regard to gearboxes; and Stirling tended to change mounts too much, so that he lacked the continuous development and the depth of knowledge built up when a driver is a regular member of a team.

Stirling tried a works BRM at Goodwood the day after the Easter Monday meeting. He loved the machine straight away and after trying all three of the works cars he picked the one that Harry Schell had been driving. Straight away he achieved the first 100 mph lap of Goodwood and considered the handling to be first class. He drove for us at Silverstone in the International Trophy, but some very foolish mistakes were made at Bourne. Stirling received some wrong information and was not given the car he had picked. Although he led the race for the first few laps, the brakes failed completely and he had to spin off on to the grass and retire. He was furious and that was the end of his driving for BRM.

The show model Cooper-Bristol the author drove at Goodwood.

I still felt that we could achieve everything if only Moss was driving the right BRM. Stirling Moss's father, Alfred and his manager, Ken Gregory, had formed a small private team called British Racing Partnership. BRP usually ran one or two Cooper-Climaxes, had various drivers and a very good chief mechanic in Tony Robinson.

Having known Alfred and Aileen Moss as friends since the time when their children, Stirling and Pat, were still young, I had a very easy relationship with them. I suggested to Alfred that they should try to borrow a BRM to be prepared by Tony Robinson, driven by Stirling and entered by BRP. Alfred Moss, Ken Gregory and Stirling all thought that this could be the answer, so I approached AGB on the project. He was prepared to try this despite some opposition from Bourne.

In due course one of the P25 BRMs was loaned to BRP for the season. This caused the only row I had with Peter Berthon and my relationship with the rest of the staff at Bourne was not

*Goodwood, 1959: Tony
Rudd, Ken Gregory and
Stirling Moss, before
Stirling's 100 mph lap.*

below:

*Silverstone paddock: Brian
Turke, Dick Geoffrey,
Carroll Shelby and Jean
Behra, with Dunlop Service.*

Sir Alfred Owen with the V16 and P25 BRMs.

too good. Raymond Mays, however, was all right about it. The car was initially prepared by the works at Bourne and finally by Tony Robinson. It was beautifully painted in Stirling's pale green and white, very like the shade of the original ERAs and V16 BRM.

All my heart was in that car. Only lack of intimate experience with the BRM prevented Moss from winning the British Grand Prix at Aintree in 1959. Moss thought it was running out of fuel. He need not have stopped and could have won. Additionally, it was only through a rare mistake that he did not figure well at Reims. Understandably, Stirling felt a lack of confidence in the

Stirling Moss in the BRP/BRM at Aintree, 1959; he should have won, but for a false indication of fuel shortage.

Sir Alfred Owen's Bentley and the author's Jaguar at Silverstone.

Launch of the BRM P25 at Raymond Mays and Partners, Bourne: Peter Berthon, Raymond Mays, Pete Collins and Sir Alfred Owen.

Above:
Impossible! Having spun at Thillois on the hot tar, Stirling tries to push-start the BRM.

Right:
Showing the new book to the boss: *The Story of the V16 BRM Engine,* **by Rivers Fletcher and Laurence Pomeroy.**

BRM, deciding to drive Rob Walker's Cooper-Climax in the next race, the German Grand Prix, at the Avus circuit near Berlin.

Hans Herrmann, a charming English-speaking German driver, drove the BRP's BRM at the Avus. His sensational accident, in which the car was written off and he was injured was caused by yet another brake failure. Talking to Hans that night in the hospital, we were immensely relieved that he was not seriously injured, but that was the end of the BRP/BRM project. The bits and pieces were returned to Bourne and quite a lot of parts were salvaged for the stores.

The Brandenburg Gate, Berlin.

Quite early one morning, against Isobel's good advice, I went through the Brandenburg Gate (this was before the Berlin wall had been built) into the Russian sector. The roads seemed deserted so I started to take some film of the scene. Suddenly I was surrounded by heavily armed police and roughly taken into a police station. I did not know their language, nor they mine. I did not have my passport with me and things looked very nasty. They took my camera away and my films. All my protestations were useless and I began to be very frightened. Eventually they found a senior Russian policeman who understood a little English. However, my story was not very convincing because, quite obviously, I had no right to be in the Russian sector at all, let alone taking film of the scene. I told him that I was with the German driver Hans Herrmann, but that did not seem to help and he had never heard of BRM.

However, to my great relief and some surprise, they escorted me back to the Brandenburg Gate and gave me back my camera and film. This was better than I deserved and so a rather frightened and foolish Rivers Fletcher returned to the safety of the Western sector. It had been no fun at all, I could easily have lost the camera and film for ever and could have been kept in the Russian sector for several days.

We have given numerous talks and film shows featuring the BRM to every sort of audience all over the British Isles, from audiences of a dozen members of Toc H in a small Welsh village to nearly a thousand of the general public at Kensington Town Hall. After a show in Dublin, I was presented with a fine large plate inscribed to "Sir Alfred Rivers-Fletcher". The civic dignitary who presented it was very nearly sober: it could only have happened in Ireland, that wonderful country, those wonderful enthusiasts.

CHAPTER TWENTY ONE

I was finding myself out of my depth in trying to win the hillclimb championship against younger and better drivers with their 1100 cc Coopers, and so I looked for something in another class. Being with BRM, I developed a great love for the $2\frac{1}{2}$-litre front-engine P25. I tried to persuade Sir Alfred Owen to let me have one of these machines for hillclimbs, but this time I pushed my luck too far and he would not go along. I thought I might persuade him to let me buy a spare car, but he was quite adamant that he did not want me racing a BRM. In retrospect, I realize that he was absolutely right. My job was to be with these cars in Formula One helping the team and he said that for my own hillclimbs I should have to buy something else.

It occurred to me that HWM had tried one of its single-seaters with a Jaguar engine and, as I already had a Jaguar Mark 2 saloon for my everyday transport, I thought it would be advantageous to have my racing car with the same engine. Through my old friend George Abecassis, (I had known him since his Cambridge days in the 1930s), I bought from Tony Gaze his Formula Two HWM. This had a $2\frac{1}{2}$-litre Alta engine with a large Shorrocks supercharger mated to a C-type Jaguar gearbox. Tony Gaze had contrived this car for hillclimbs, but did not take to this kind of event at all and that was why he was selling. I immediately sold the Alta engine and supercharger to Frank Norris as a spare for his single-seater Alta. Then I bought a $3\frac{1}{2}$-litre Jaguar engine from Stirling Moss. That of course mated up straight away with the Jaguar gearbox in the HWM.

Leslie Ballamy carried out the work and Freddie Owen modified the body, giving it higher sides and a different nose. This different appearance was justified to distinguish it from other, Alta-engined HWMs. I thought the car was excellent and I loved it. It was not madly competitive, but it gave me a most enjoyable ride, with splendid handling.

After the first season with that car I had a very bad shunt, which was entirely my fault. It happened at Prescott, on the testing day. I do not think I was really concentrating and tried to take the first fast lefthander without lifting off. I got it sideways and failed to catch it in time. The car mounted the bank and went end over end, throwing me out on to the track and bouncing partly on top of me as it landed. Altogether it was very unpleasant. The car rolled on beyond me as I lay unconscious and severely injured in the middle of the track. My crash helmet was nearly split in two and I had nasty-looking head injuries. I was rushed to hospital and all concerned were marvellous – as they always are.

There were no bones broken but severe concussion seemed to pose problems. After our own team and family, my first visitor was Donald Monro, who came straight from London and then David Boshier-Jones from Monmouth. For several weeks I was in a vague state of mind, unable to think or speak coherently.

Specialists at the Hospital of Nervous Diseases in London carried out numerous tests and I was wired up to very sophisticated apparatus. Still my speech was very hesitant.

Below far left:
Freddie Owen, Leslie Ballamy and Isobel with the HWM, minus engine, at Guildford.

Below:
Isobel in wet weather garb all ready to be towed to Freddie Owen's for coachbuilding.

Perhaps fortunately, I had absolutely no memory of the accident itself. I grew a beard to hide some of the scars and went back to work far too early where I was no help at all, but just a burden. By far the most distressing effect of my shunt was that under any amount of stress my speech disappeared completely; worse still - I could not understand a word said to me. It was as if all speech to me and from me, was in unscrambled code.

Very frightened that I was becoming mentally ill, I tried to hide my problems. Carrying on my work in the Owen Organisation made Isobel's job almost impossible. After some frightening blackout sessions I was terrified that I would be put in an asylum. I still wonder what sort of rubbish I probably spoke at several meetings before I was led away to rest – not a happy period in my life.

As soon as the HWM Jaguar was repaired I returned to the hillclimbs but my doctor would not give me a certificate for racing on circuits. Penny and Isobel did most of the talking for me. Only once at a Prescott hillclimb did the doctor in charge query my fitness to drive; but since my practice times were up to scratch, I was passed OK.

Jaguar in the HWM.

Above:
HWM-Jaguar, Prescott.

right:
**Penny ready for Prescott with
the Sprite Minor 1000.**

Below:
**After the author's accident:
the steering wheel and
cockpit.**

In due course Isobel was going into her family business and before that there were plans for extending her experience. All this had been in the pipeline before my accident. Now, with great generosity, Isobel decided that she would stay on until I was recovered. She did this with AGB's blessing and help. I can never thank them enough; no other boss would have had such patience and I do not like to think what problems and responsibilities Isobel must have faced. I was in a pretty poor shape, although slowly getting better. AGB even sent me off to America, there and back on the *Queen Elizabeth*, just to look at an exhibition in New York. "I don't want a report" he said. "Just regard it as a holiday to get well". Although the workload was growing all the time, Isobel coped with everything at Kent House.

HWM-Jaguar in the paddock at Prescott; Doc Taylor with 'Alfi' in the background.

I carried on my work as PRO of the Owen organization and BRM - but I could not have been much good and I remember little of it now. Everyone was most helpful and considerate. AGB never pushed me and good friends like Stirling Moss, Rob Walker, Raymond Baxter, as well as most of the Press, dealt with me via Isobel.

One of the greatest races we covered, although it was not a good one for BRM, was the 1960 Monaco Grand Prix, where we saw Stirling Moss driving Rob Walker's Lotus-Climax near the limit all the way, winning that race from Bruce McLaren's Cooper.

Isobel tries Doc Taylor's special 'Alfi' and Tony Taylor gives a push-start. Doug Wilcox beside the car.

Below far right:
On the Rubery Owen stand at Earls Court – showing Norman Wisdom.

Below:
At the racing car show: Giulio Ramponi explains to the author how he rebuilt the 1½-litre Delage for Dick Seaman.

In June 1961, AGB became Sir Alfred, a knighthood richly deserved. Many people in our world of motor racing believed that he had been knighted just for BRM, albeit deservedly. Few realized the prodigious amount of his good work for a much wider public: besides help to various religious denominations, there was every sort of welfare and aid for orphans, the sick, the unemployed, the handicapped and prisoners. He was the senior executive in many welfare organizations, including Dr Barnado's Homes, of which he was Chairman. It was AGB who brought Billy Graham, the American evangelist, over here.

I could write so many stories about Sir Alfred: this little incident is typical. He kept a few pigs on the farmland adjacent to Sutton Grange, where his mother lived. Sometimes, when there

was a binful of waste food in the main canteen at the works Sir Alfred would put it in the boot of his Bentley and take it back for his pigs.

There was a new girl working in the canteen kitchen. One morning, Sir Alfred came in with an empty bin in his arms and dumped it down in the kitchen. Just as he was going out the girl, who had not seen him before, shouted after him, "Come back at once: I won't have your dirty dustbin in my clean kitchen. Pick it up and put it outside." Sir Alfred immediately apologized and removed it.

Needless to say, the girl could not believe it when she was told that he was Sir Alfred, the Chairman. The real point of the story is that Sir Alfred himself did not even notice this aspect of the situation: he knew he should not have put the bin in the kitchen and the girl was quite right.

On the death of Sir Malcolm Campbell – quite peacefully in bed, after so many years of hair-raising escapes with his Bluebird racing cars – his son Donald announced that he would go for the land speed record in a new jet-propelled Bluebird. I had known Donald since he was a little boy, but had not thought he would become involved in this sort of game. I wrote to him wishing him good luck and said that I was sure that Sir Alfred would like to help by providing parts and perhaps by doing a bit of

Monaco GP 1960, first corner: Jo Bonnier (BRM) leads, followed by Brabham (works Cooper), Brooks and Bristow (BRP-Cooper), with Stirling Moss (Walker/Lotus) inside then Phil Hill (Ferrari), and Innes Ireland outside (Lotus). Coming into the corner very close are Graham Hill (BRM) alongside Surtees (Lotus) and Ginther (Ferrari). Ahead of them is von Trips (Ferrari), locking over. Then come Salvadori and McLaren (Coopers), Gurney (BRM) and Trintignant (Cooper-Maserati). Isobel can be seen filming: she is the seventh person from the right, in flowered dress, by the straw bales.

machining from time to time at companies in our group. Instead of getting just a polite letter back, I received an immediate invitation to lunch at Claridges: which I thought significant, remembering his dear father who, of course, I had idolized when I was very young. Over lunch, Donald dropped his bombshell saying, "Rivers, this is a wonderful opportunity for you and the Owen organization. You could build Bluebird in one of your works".

I knew this was out of the question, so I explained how completely impossible this would be. We were already expending far too much money and effort on BRM and Sir Alfred was finding it increasingly difficult to persuade his own companies to support any sort of motor racing. The most we could do would be to provide a little assistance with nuts and bolts and some machining.

Donald understood, but said he would like to meet Sir Alfred, so I arranged this. I immediately wrote at length to Donald, confirming to him how impossible it would be for us to build the car. I sent a copy of the letter to Sir Alfred and also wrote him a memo, warning him and assuring him that I had said a firm "No" to Donald.

When Sir Alfred came into my office, before he went to meet Donald, he said to me, "I do hope you made it quite clear to Donald that we could never consider making Bluebird. You know what the other directors will say, even if we give him nuts and bolts". I assured him that I had.

About two hours later, a rather sheepish Sir Alfred told me that we were going to build Bluebird at Motor Panels at Coventry, one of our large companies. It was a long and complicated story, with plenty of drama. We built Bluebird and Donald wrote it off. As expected, the other directors were not amused. And, of course, it was largely Rivers' fault – what a PRO! First of all BRM and now Bluebird – nothing but dead losses. Then to cap it all, Sir Alfred decided that we would

Bluebird under construction for Donald Campbell at Motor Panels Ltd, Coventry – where they did it all again after Donald's accident.

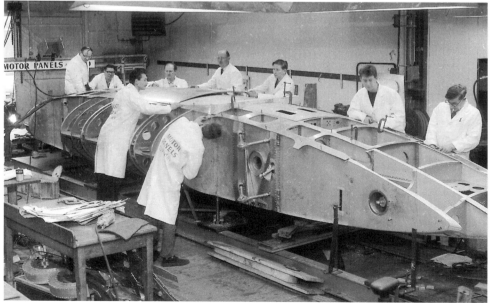

rebuild Bluebird because he thought we should try to get the land speed record for Donald, as well as the World Championship with BRM for Raymond Mays – and all for Great Britain.

Isobel had carried me and the job for about 18 months. Only then, when I had seemed much fitter and better able to cope and when she had organized a promising replacement secretary, did Isobel leave after 10 years. Under trying conditions Jennie Goodsall, my new secretary managed the job well and was very understanding of my continuing speech difficulties. Although Isobel's new job took her out of England part of the time, she kept in touch and helped considerably when possible.

For BRM 1962 was roses all the way. Peter Berthon's 1½-litre V8 engine was right first time. At AGB's instigation we had a splendid little two-car team with Graham Hill and Ritchie Ginther, together with Tony Rudd as team manager.

It was to be a make-or-break year and Sir Alfred insisted on the cars being all-British. That meant a new Lucas ignition system. He told me that if we were to be successful he wanted a film to show the world. I therefore got two film companies to quote for the job; I would just provide extra footage this time. As I expected, the costs were astronomical compared with the films we ourselves had made previously. Sir Alfred smiled and told me to go ahead and make the film as in the past. However, he expected it to be as good as any professionally-made film and no more expensive than our previous efforts.

Donald Campbell, Leo Villa and Tonia with Bluebird before the Press demonstration at Goodwood.

This was typical of him and I loved his confidence and the challenge. Although she was employed by another company abroad, I said that I wanted Isobel back to operate the second camera when possible, also warning Sir Alfred that I would have to be away on the Continent most of the summer. He agreed everything, but again warned me that he expected a first-class result.

Sir Alfred Owen wins the 1962 Ferodo Trophy. At the Dorchester Hotel in London are: Ronald Pochin, Managing Director of Ferodo; Sir Alfred; Peter Berthon; and Raymond Mays in the V16 BRM.

I drove to the first event, the Brussels Grand Prix, in my Mark 2 Jaguar and Isobel flew in from Paris in time for the first practice session. Graham Hill won this event and continued to win throughout the season, but only just stayed ahead of Jim Clark for the championship. It was Hill again at Goodwood on Easter Monday, when Stirling Moss had the tragic shunt that finished his Grand Prix career. We filmed Graham's victory in the Dutch GP at Zandvoort, and his lucky second place at Spa, where Isobel filmed the sensational collision of Willy Mairesse and Trevor Taylor. At Monaco, Penny took the second camera and had to film some dreadful incidents at very close range. Her shots of the first-lap multiple accident at the Gasworks hairpin were dramatic, (a flying wheel seriously injured an official by her side and he died later).

For the German Grand Prix at the Nürburgring, which

Graham won in pouring rain, the second camera was taken by Pamela Ferris, whose experience had been as private secretary to Sir John Hodge. The latter was an old friend who used to race a Le Mans Singer at Brooklands. The Nürburgring is really too long for just two cameras, but we covered the essential victory despite the appalling conditions.

Over the previous months my speech and my mind had been improving, but very slowly. In every direction I was being helped. Nevertheless, people cannot keep on making allowances for ever

Earl Howe, and Graham Hill in the winning BRM with the Ferodo Trophy, and Sir Alfred Owen.

and halfway through 1962, after the British Grand Prix at Aintree, which we did not win, I came to pieces and "lost my prop". That is the only way I can describe my complete loss of confidence. Something inside me snapped. Other people did not know of course, but from that time on my state of mind kept on slipping; no sooner had I gained a little confidence than I quickly lost more.

It might have been thought that the first months, certainly the first year or so, after my injuries would be the worst period. That was not the case. The first year or so was the best period, with everyone making allowances and helping me. Then suddenly I felt alone with myself and unsure if I could cope.

I realize now that much of my behaviour after the middle of 1962 was appalling: I was seeking comfort and support, wanting someone to hold my hand when I should have been pulling myself together. Thankfully, Penny at home and my new secretary, Pamela Ferris at work, took a firm hand with me. I know it was difficult for Penny, but she did the right thing. For Pamela and the rest of my small staff at Kent House I must have been a terrible problem. They coped very well for another four or five years without any great disasters. From time to time my

At the NLECC dinner, left to right: Gregor Grant, Pat Taylor, Penny, Henry Taylor, the author, John Eason-Gibson, Raymond Baxter, Mrs Baxter, Colin Chapman, Hazel Chapman.

speech almost disappeared again. At my favourite Great Auclum and at one Prescott hillclimb I had to withdraw from the racing, scared that I might have a blackout and on the road I was very careful when I was going through a bad patch.

Absolutely determined to conquer this problem and somehow believing that everything would be right again one day, I continued to give some talks and film shows. I believe that my speech was still too halting, but these efforts of mine cannot have been too bad. It is with a sense of shame that I have to admit that my job for the Owen organization suffered. A big London Group dinner, for example, did not go as smoothly as it should have done. I shall never know how Sir Alfred put up with my inefficiency for such a long time, but he did.

In the very last days of 1962, between Christmas and New Year 1963, the BRM achieved its crowning victory with Graham Hill's win in the South African Grand Prix; the first all-British car ever to win the World Championship and with a British driver. Thank heaven that event was on a Saturday so Sir Alfred was able to attend and witness the great occasion.

That evening we sat together before the prize-giving ceremony and I think our hearts were too full for words. We kept on grinning at one another. We did not normally shake hands when we said good night, but on this occasion AGB held my hand for a long time and said, "We knew that we would win one day".

That plural pronoun was not absolutely justifiable, because over the years I did have many doubts; it was only Sir Alfred who was completely steadfast.

CHAPTER TWENTY TWO

As holder of the World Championship, BRM was welcomed everywhere. I had an engineless mock-up BRM, which I carted around for exhibition with my film of the races. In all the group companies, our engineers and salesmen used BRM to advantage. In Czechoslovakia and Poland, behind the Iron Curtain as it then was, as well as in all the English-speaking countries of the world, we staged exhibitions, held seminars and showed the flag.

Of all the racing events, those that I enjoyed most took place in the long stint covering the South African Grand Prix, the Tasman Series of four races in New Zealand and another four in Australia. In this way, I was in the hot sun of the Southern Hemisphere through most of December, January and February, when it was cold and wet in Britain.

The very best of that series was the 1966 Tasman Cup. The BRM team was managed by Reg Parnell's son, Tim. By this time we had our new young Scottish ace Jackie Stewart and World Champion Graham Hill, on occasions supported by Dickie Attwood. Since our group had large engineering companies in Australia, it was very apt that we had such success in that part of the world. Jackie Stewart dominated the series, very sportingly supported by Graham. The Tasman Cup was Jackie Stewart's first really big international success and came before he won the World Championship.

It was delightful to be out there in the happy, relaxed atmosphere of motor racing in New Zealand and Australia, especially since Grands Prix elsewhere, and BRM's involvement in them in particular, were becoming ever more deadly serious – and not always pleasantly so.

At the conclusion of that Tasman Series I took the victorious BRM to Hong Kong, where the British Government showed it as a star exhibit in British Week. Sir Alfred flew over to present the car to Princess Margaret and Lord Snowdon. This was very appropriate because at the time the group was involved in the production of a new invalid carriage sponsored by Lord Snowdon.

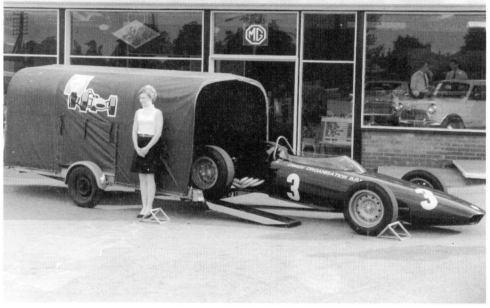

Also in the mid-1960s, Graham Hill in his BRM V8 absolutely dominated the Monaco Grand Prix for three years, winning in 1963-6. In addition, BRM was runner-up to Jim Clark and Lotus in the World Championship in 1963.

The H16 BRM was another bold venture. Tony Rudd was as right as Peter Berthon had been with the V16 unit – in theory. In practice the complication multiplied the possible mistakes. It seemed, therefore, that without a large slice of luck, which seldom came BRM's way, simpler power units were more successful. Innovating again, we produced a four-wheel-drive BRM which Ritchie Ginther tested extensively. Like other four-wheel-drive Formula One cars, it was quite successful. However, the advent of very large sticky tyres made the complication and extra weight of 4WD unnecessary.

Sir Alfred and Ritchie Ginther at Oulton Park; Elizabeth Owen films from the pits.

BRM preparation in New South Wales, Australia, for the Tasman Series.

Right:
My favourite photograph of
Sir Alfred Owen.

Far right:
Sir Alfred shows the
successful BRM to Princess
Margaret in Hong Kong,
1963.

Right:
Practice at Silverstone;
Tony Rudd behind the car,
while Graham cuts a slice of
sorbo for more backrest.

Below:
Jackie with the Tasman
Trophy and Helen, after
winning the final race at
Sandown, 1963.

Above:
Jackie Stewart in the H16 BRM, with Graham Hill, Cyril Atkins, Willie Southgate, Tony Rudd, Sir Alfred Owen and Raymond Mays.

Four-wheel-drive BRM.

Donald Campbell took the land speed record in the rebuilt Bluebird, so Sir Alfred and the Owen organization were on top of the world: moreover the Group was growing and prospering magnificently.

The gas-turbine Rover-BRM of 1963 was a very successful venture, at a time when both companies were doing very well in their respective fields. Our drivers Graham Hill and Ritchie Ginther however, were not all that keen on the project. Graham Hill's comment was, "an unproved and probably very slow car in a very long drag".

Matra-BRM at Le Mans. The gas turbine Rover-BRM was entered for the 1963 Le Mans. As neither company was a regular Le Mans competitor, hotel and other accommodation was difficult. I had no complaints at all in a nurses' hostel and refused to swap it with our drivers' luxury hotel. Wilkie Wilkinson with his great Jaguar Le Mans experience managed the team and with little difficulty our Rover-BRM achieved the object: the special trophy for the first successful gas-turbine entry at Le Mans. Two years later a development of that car, driven by Graham Hill and Jackie Stewart, achieved even more and was the first British car to finish in the 1965 Le Mans.

Sir Alfred's work for the welfare of prisoners and their families and for the rehabilitation of offenders, fitted in well with my previous experience with the Vice Squad at Scotland Yard. I became a regular prison visitor and gave my shows at all the

London and Midland prisons. Both Stirling Moss and I became honorary members of the Maidstone Jail Motor Club. The prison governor said he hoped Stirling would not be roped in for a future fast escape!

In the mid-1960s, Rubery Owen was involved with Matra in France with missiles and aerospace projects. This association led to the Matra-BRMs entered in the 1966 Le Mans and a Matra coupé for my use. For Le Mans, we used the 2-litre V8 BRM engine in very light Matra coupés. I dealt with Gerard Ducarouge and Jean Lagardère of Matra and we had a good team of drivers, mostly French, for a three-car team. Wilkie Wilkinson and Arthur Hill of BRM were seconded to Matra. The cars ran well enough but without achieving any great results. During one of the testing sessions we had a tragic accident when Robey Webber lost control on the Mulsanne Straight. The car was completely destroyed and Robey was killed instantly. Wilkie had been worried about the aerodynamics of the cars, fearing that their tails would lift at high speed. There were plans to modify the design but, sadly, this was not completed in time for the tests.

My son Peter working on his Turner beside the single-seater Jaguar.

The 1½-litre and 1100 HRGs at home; my son Jeremy on the 1100.

After a lot of Bentley, Jaguar and Jaguar-engined racing, I found myself looking at the very smallest racing cars of all: machines not much bigger than karts. My younger son Jeremy, when he was about 14, had a lot of fun with his Trokart and I enjoyed it too, racing round the garden. I had been watching Peter Wilson with his little Martin Special at Prescott and noted his tremendous performance on the Bouley Bay hillclimb. I thought it would be rather fun to make a new car in that category. I discussed the project with Leslie Ballamy, always an innovator. I had so much enjoyed driving his supercharged LMB Ford Popular saloon and I knew he would be enthusiastic about a new project. We both knew Mike Luff who built the Buckler Specials at Crowthorne. I borrowed a Buckler kart from Mike

Above right:
With Mike Luff; the BB Special under construction, showing the position of the nose.

Above left:
Breaking the saloon record at Great Auclum in Leslie Ballamy's supercharged LMB Ford Popular.

for the Bugatti Owners' Club testing day at Prescott. It was quite good fun, but did not feel like motor racing. However, our project was going to be a real miniature formula racing car. We called it the BB Special, (for Ballamy and Buckler). The design was a joint effort with a very ingenious steering gear layout by Leslie. It was nearly ready, but without a body, when I foolishly ran it at Great Auclum. We had a rather disastrous day. The gearing was all wrong, but Leslie's steering seemed fine. What saved the day for me was the fact that I also drove my 1½-litre HRG, which ran well.

The real sensation of the event was Isobel driving her Cooper-Norton 500. Her first run time was recorded as a good deal faster than seemed possible. It was much quicker than Patsy Burt, who was normally fastest lady. Isobel herself did not believe the recorded time. She very sportingly agreed to having that run again, which disallowed her record performance. Her re-run was good, quite up to her normal standard, but nothing like that record. All of us, particularly Patsy Burt, applauded Isobel's sporting gesture. Few other people would have taken that action, I believe, but it was typical of her.

Now the BB was ready for the next Prescott with a beautiful little body made by Freddie Owen, who also built a lovely small trailer for it. The workmanship was superb and on the hill it handled well. However, it was soon obvious that the little 250 cc Bultaco engine was nothing like powerful enough.

The single-seater Jaguar leaving the line at Great Auclum: wheelspin from both rear wheels with the new limited slip differential.

Isobel driving her Cooper-Norton at Ettore's Bend, Prescott.

Above:
Isobel going up to the line at Chateau Impney.

Above right:
The BB Special: Freddie Owen with the little car on the trailer behind the author's Mark II Jaguar.

Freddie Owen had considerable motorcycle racing experience and knew how to get hold of a good Triumph Tiger Twin engine, which he said would be just the job. Like all these things, it took more time than we thought and the season was over by the time it was ready. Off to an airfield in the autumn we found there was plenty of urge low down but it soon ran out of steam. Further tests convinced me that the BB Special would never be fast enough for the long Prescott hillclimb and hopeless at Shelsley Walsh, but I believed that it might be exactly right for the very short and twisty Great Auclum. In previous years I had achieved second fastest time of the day there with my Cooper-JAP. Now I pictured myself flying round the first corner on the lip of the banking and throwing the little BB up the hill at record speed – or so I imagined!

I put in my entry for Great Auclum. About ten days before the event the BB Special was on a soapbox, its wheels off being balanced. The car was in the big barn at the end of my garden. It was a warm summer evening, Penny was at a rehearsal for a play in the amateur dramatic society. A friend of mine came over for a chat and we were sitting on the terrace drinking coffee.

At the wheel of the BB Special; Isobel behind the car.

There was a faint soft breeze blowing wisps of smoke from a bonfire at the bottom of my neighbour's garden. Too bad we thought; his gardener had no right to leave the bonfire burning in the evening.

For quite a time we lazily watched the smoke curling up into the sky. Then my friend said, "It's getting worse" and we could hear it crackling. Suddenly I realized it was not a bonfire. The smoke was coming from my barn. We ran like mad and, as I opened the big doors, there was a great whoosh and flames filled that side of the barn. We could not get near the BB Special and even if we had been able to do so, I doubt if we could have got it out without its wheels. There was one other car in the barn on the other side, my Mark 2 Jaguar. We opened the other door, I leaped in and backed the Jaguar out just before the whole place was engulfed in flames.

There was absolutely nothing that we could do. I dashed back to the house and rang the Fire Brigade. Someone else had seen the flames, however, and I was told that the engine was on its way. It was quite a blaze because there was a lot of hay in the loft. The firemen got water from a nearby hydrant and from the pond beyond the barn. The fire was soon under control, so nearby trees and fencing were undamaged, but my lovely old barn, the BB Special and a good deal of racing equipment were destroyed. Only the foundation and stone floors remained. Penny

The author's much-modified Mark II Jaguar, with the little BB Special, at the back of the racing stable at Arkley.

returned from her rehearsal to find at home: two fire engines, numbers of policemen and a happily unnecessary ambulance.

The police first thought that the fire had been started by someone sleeping rough in the loft over the barn, because we had reported seeing a tramp there. The Fire Brigade, however, told us that it was caused by "spontaneous combustion" in the hay packed tightly in the loft. They explained how such things happen – and in fact the Fire Brigade had to be recalled early the next morning because the hay from the loft started burning again.

The insurance people were more than helpful and even generous. Spontaneous combustion is classed as an act of God and so was not covered by my insurance. However, the insurance assessor said that the Fire Brigade could not be absolutely certain of the cause of fire, so the company paid up despite having a good excuse for not doing so.

I had no desire to go further with the tiny racing project although, seen in retrospect, it was quite good fun and good experience. Penny is convinced that the only spectacular thing I would have done at Great Auclum would have been to fly over the top of that banking. Perhaps it was just as well I did not try. I still was not all that fit and had not regained my full confidence. I was still frightened of loss of speech and entirely dependent on sleeping pills each night: not the right conditions for any sort of motor racing.

My next acquisition was a more orthodox racing car, a single-seater Jaguar which Bill Moss built for me. Then I bought two more HRGs, with which I was to have some racing.

Pressures of a new kind were being felt in BRM. The sad death of AGB's younger brother Ernest left the Chairman

Freddie Owen building the body for the author's single-seater Jaguar.

The big single-seater Jaguar on Pardon Hairpin, Prescott.

without his valuable support. Ernest was the kindest of men, always most considerate to me, supportive of BRM and all his brother's many other activities.

The impossibly arduous amount of work that AGB undertook was taking its toll. He became sick, really very sick, but would not reduce his workload and stubbornly refused to take a proper holiday. Inevitably BRM suffered, as other things did. Eventually AGB suffered a mild stroke and then a much more severe one. My job, in which I had been so happy under his sole direction, became very difficult.

I now felt that I had to be on my own and set up as a consultant. Reluctantly, I therefore asked to be released from my position with the Owen organization, giving six-months' notice. AGB was wonderful and told me that my job was safe for ever, but he understood the situation and gave me all the leave and help I required during my last six months.

I often look back with fond memories on my time working with Sir Alfred Owen. He was always inclined to make too many appointments, particularly for his London visits. So I was often

NLECC annual dinner and dance – not really the band, with Gregor Grant, Raymond Baxter and Colin Chapman.

required to take his place, no doubt to the disappointment of some important people at his meetings, luncheons, dinners or sometimes just 'à deux'.

On occasions I represented Sir Alfred speaking for him to leading politicians such as Reginald Maudling, Nye Bevan, Tom Driberg and Robert Boothby, and to heads of companies like Sir Charles Forte and Sir Bernard Docker and personalities like Billy Graham, Godfrey Winn and others. I had to answer questions on Sir Alfred's unusual Christian administration of his companies, the justification of the BRM racing car, Dr. Barnardo's Homes, and the rapid growth of the Owen Organisation which had become the largest privately owned company in Britain.

Some of those to whom I spoke already knew Sir Alfred quite well, including Billy Graham and Charles Forte, but some others did not know him personally. Everyone was fascinated by the paternalistic Rubery Owen management which was a strange mixture of old and new ideas. Only Reginald Maudling (who happened to be my local MP) and Nye Bevan expressed doubts as to whether such an altruistic management structure could be sustained in future years. Interesting – because they reasoned, of course, from opposing political viewpoints. Again, as the representative of Sir Alfred I had to remember that he was not really 'party political', but rather 'above it' though he himself would, of course, deny it. Rank, title or fame made no impression on him – he gave the same attention to all.

Perhaps irreverantly, I describe Sir Alfred as a 'Hot Gospeller', certainly an Evangelist, more 'Chapel' than Church of England (although again he would not agree), low church rather than high. Moving as he did in such a wide circle – industry, religion, sport, politics and charities, etc., I worried how his strict non-conformist teetotal and religion-bound attitudes could fit in. I need not have been concerned – he just sailed through everything with happy, smiling confidence.

For me it was sometimes more difficult. For example, I took Tom Driberg to lunch, on Sir Alfred's instructions. I chose a good, but not madly expensive, restaurant in Soho. Driberg had an apéritif, a bottle of wine and a liqueur whilst I was content with my usual glass of orange. No problems; I answered all his questions and he was most interested in the way or group was managed. My expenses were paid, but in a memo Sir Alfred complained of the large amount and high cost of the drink. It so happened that this occurred just before an Easter Monday race meeting at Goodwood where we were racing the BRMs. Meeting Sir Alfred in the Pits at the start of the meeting, he cheerfully asked me if I had a happy Easter. I said that I was sorry to say that I had had a very unhappy Easter. He asked me why and I told him that I was very upset to get his memo because I tried so hard to do the right thing and I cared so much to no avail.

He said that he had no recollection of the memo; he signed dozens every day. From time to time, they had a blitz on expenses. Probably the one to me was just one in a batch typed by his secretary, Miss Ramsden. He forthwith gave me a good 'talking to' – told me I was too sensitive, and with so many people and situations to deal with, he couldn't for ever be worried if that someone felt he was sometimes being wrongly or over-criticized.

I felt better but also rather a fool as well. Sir Alfred really was an amazing man, so steadfast in his beliefs – yet so talented and understanding. Over the years we developed a great and sincere affection for one another, enabling us to discuss many personal matters usually beyond the realm of our situation. I will always be grateful to have had such a boss for such a long and important time in my life.

The very human and personal content in our BRM films gave Sir Alfred the idea of making films for his religious and charitable activities. So the Owen organization Film Unit (only Isobel and myself – union rules flouted!) made 16 mm colour sound films for Dr Barnardo's; for boys' camps at Lillishall featuring the famous county cricketer David Shepherd (later the Bishop of Liverpool), boys mountaineering in Wales featuring Sir John Hunt, and religious pop music featuring two guitar-strumming young clergymen calling themselves "the Rock and Roll Parsons".

Our lives couldn't have been more varied. Once when David Shepherd and I were staying with Sir Alfred, we were driving back on a dark and wet night from Evensong. Sir Alfred was driving us in his Mark VI Bentley and we had a puncture. Somehow or other, it was Sir Alfred who did all the dirty work, getting the jack underneath the car and dealing with the filthy wheel, whilst David and I undid nuts and handled the clean spare wheel. Quite typical that only Sir Alfred had dirty hands and muck on his trousers. I bet any other millionaire industrialist would have sat in the car whilst we did all the work.

Sir Alfred was much in demand as a preacher, speaking to very large congregations in Birmingham and London; I personally

At Spa Trevor Taylor walks away uninjured from another shunted Lotus.

thought his sermons too long. On one occasion staying with Sir Alfred, we went to a little village and Sir Alfred preached his sermon only to a handful of old ladies. I though it was a shocking waste of his talent, and said so. I had a stab at suggesting that the Bible preached the Gospel to the widest public and that the Word of God would be used more efficently to a larger congregation of younger people. Sir Alfred just smiled and told me that if I knew the Scriptures better, I would understand that the little group of old ladies was just as important to God as a much larger congregatiuon of young people. I was put in my place, but kindly.

The parting was sad in a way, but the timing was right. BRM was changing and both Tony Rudd and Graham Hill moved to Lotus. I was not only leaving BRM, I was also quitting Formula One altogether. I knew it was no longer my scene. Heavy sponsorship was on the way, with advertisements all over the cars. The names of makes of cars were being replaced by those of brands of cigarettes and cosmetics. What I had grown up with as a sport was becoming big business. Sporting standards were going.

I could not really grumble. I had enjoyed a lion's share of what was to me the greatest sport in the world. Now, just at the right time for me, vintage, historic and what we now call classic, motor racing was blooming.

My heart was already there, so it was with the greatest of ease that I turned away from Grands Prix and towards the vintage scene.

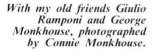

With my old friends Giulio Ramponi and George Monkhouse, photographed by Connie Monkhouse.

PART VI

NEW HORIZONS

On my own as a consultant.
Vintage and historic racing and
good future prospects.

CHAPTER TWENTY THREE

Leaving the Owen group and setting myself up as a consultant gave me a good excuse for leaving the Home Counties altogether. Barnet, Totteridge and Arkley had once been country, but the London suburbs had spread and swallowed them; now there were too many houses, too many cars and far too many people.

My first thoughts were to the Norfolk Broads, where my relaxation was motor cruising. I then realized that the Broads were too far out of the mainstream. I had to consider somewhere close to the middle of England, with reasonable access to Coventry, Birmingham, the Midlands in general, London and, most importantly, Silverstone, Shelsley Walsh, Prescott and Donington.

For much of my work for the Owen organization and BRM I had stayed at the Alveston Manor Hotel in Stratford-upon-Avon. I came to love the place and the countryside about. I soon found a suitable old house in the village of Kineton, on the edge of the Cotswolds, about ten miles from Stratford.

My fears and worries about my speech defects quickly faded away. I liked the new environment and being free from BRM problems, which had increased greatly during the last year or so. I came to realize that my occasional speech difficulty was hardly noticed by other people and was no real disadvantage. In fact, on one occasion in company with a number of motor racing people, when I was tired at the end of a long day, Innes Ireland came up to me and said, "I think I'll try your hesitant speech voice: very effective, old boy! I'm sure I could use it to my advantage, and I only wish one of my accidents could have produced the same effect".

My first job in my new consultancy role was with the Serck group at Birmingham, with my friend, Tony Rippon, the company secretary. It was perhaps not altogether my scene, but promising nevertheless. There would be not quite so much foreign travel, but some interesting visits to countries that I had not come to know via the Grand Prix circuit. Tony was a great Bugatti man and later Chairman of the Bugatti Owners' Club and, in effect, the founder of the Ferrari Owners' Club. I owe

him a great debt of gratitude for his kindness and understanding. For through him, Serck gave me full employment as public relations consultant for a couple of years – though I reckon I was really unemployable, having been spoiled by Alfred Owen.

I expected unreasonable privileges and too much autonomy. Tony Rippon and a very good secretary, Marris, gave me every help and encouragement; but at Serck the motor racing content was never enough for me. The Groups were so different. In Serck I was told, "Don't rock the boat". In the Owen organization, AGB encouraged and expected me to rock the boat: new ideas, new activities, the unpopular and dangerous BRM where stakes were high, but we were encouraged to go for them.

After Serck I diversified my activities, dividing my time between promoting a new motor journal called *Thoroughbred & Classic Cars* and the J C Bamford Group, where Anthony Bamford had a splendid collection of vintage racing cars. He gave me some of my best drives, in the ex-Malcolm Campbell Delage with Leo Villa himself in attendance and in a lovely

Above left:
Isobel Robinson in Tony Rippon's Bugatti Type 35 with the car's owner and John Willis.

Above right
Driving the Ferrari 625 for Anthony Bamford at Prescott, and winning for him the Walters-Dowell Trophy for the fastest Ferrari climb of the year.

Neil Corner in the ex-Earl Howe Bugatti Type 59 at Oulton Park.

Elizabeth Junek with Tony Rippon in Tony's Brescia Bugatti.

Ferrari 625 with which I won for him the Walters-Dowell Trophy for the fastest Ferrari climb of the year at Prescott. Then, as consultant to Shell, I gave my talks and film shows all over the country.

Having left the Grand Prix scene, I was able to attend all the vintage events. These were multiplying and growing in importance all the time. The relaxed sporting atmosphere was everything I had loved in racing before the Second World War and soon after. The racing events were enlivened by a splendid team of commentators: Tony Rippon, "Bunny" Tubbs, John Willis and James Tilling; their dry wit and knowledgeable backchat typified the vintage scene. I came to know John Willis very well. His encyclopaedic knowledge of old cars and a very amusing turn of phrase made him a delightful companion. John was the treasurer of the Bugatti Owners' Club, so we were both members of its council. I drove my single-seater Jaguar and other cars at all the Prescott meetings of the Bugatti Owners' Club, where John was the regular commentator.

In much the same way as I had lost interest in Grand Prix competition both John and I found we had little love for the new trends in cars for speed hillclimbs. Inevitably, the new machines were developing on similar lines to GP models. Our interest therefore narrowed to the classic categories and vintage meetings, where John's special expertise as commentator was so well appreciated.

Penny and the dogs, the $4\frac{1}{4}$-litre Bentley and Jeremy preparing the car at Kineton.

Above:
E R Hall tries the author's near-replica of his 4¼-litre Bentley.

Shelsley Walsh in the Bentley 4¼ TT replica.

Penny, Jeremy and some girlfriends with the R-type Bentley Continental and the TT racing Bentley on the trailer at Kineton.

Below:
The author, the 4¼ TT Bentley and the standard R-type at Kineton.

John Willis with his Alvis 12/60 at Brooklands, with Isobel, Russell Wilson-Kitchen, Bill Boddy and Leslie Ballamy.

It was not really surprising that my next competition car after the single-seater Jaguar was a pre-war model eligible for vintage events. It was my friendship with E R Hall that led me to produce a near-replica of his TT model Derby Bentley. My younger son Jeremy was serving his motor trade apprenticeship in the Rolls-Royce and Bentley agencies of Mann-Egerton in Derby and he took charge of the considerable work they did on that car.

My $4\frac{1}{4}$-litre TT type was particularly good at Shelsley Walsh, for which it happened to be ideally geared. It was never so good at Prescott, but I loved the car and soon completed my Bentley stable with a fine R-type Continental coupé by Park Ward, which John Willis found for me. I had known that car all its life, because the first owner was Jack Dunfee and he had sold it to Tony Vandervell. Another fine Bentley, which I kept for a long time, was a standard R-type saloon.

Isobel Robinson had sold her Cooper-Norton when she worked abroad for a time. Then she raced a Lotus occasionally and had a very good drive at Prescott in Tony Rippon's Bugatti Type 35. With so much motor racing experience behind her, she was of great help to John Willis when he was commentating at events. It was no surprise, and the greatest pleasure to us all, that Isobel became Mrs John Willis. So Penny and I joined them as a foursome for our favourite meetings.

My consultancy developed apace and I made films for the Vintage Sports Car Club and several companies. I gave more talks and film shows in this country, which led to shows abroad

Above:
The Stratford-upon-Avon Motor Museum, with the author's Alvis Speed 25 and Bill's Rolls-Royce Phantom I and 12-cylinder Hispano-Suiza.

Above far right:
Inside the Stratford-upon-Avon Museum: Bill Meredith-Owens poses with his own Flying Flea.

Below:
John and Isobel Willis with their Amilcar and Leslie Ballamy at Brooklands.

and all sorts of promotions, articles and books. With Bill Meredith-Owens, we set up the Stratford-upon-Avon Motor Museum, mostly with Bill's Rolls-Royces and Hispano-Suizas from India, but I brought in some racing cars.

In 1981, the whole of BRM was closed down and the cars and everything else sold. I felt a pang of sorrow because we had enjoyed some good times with the old cars, the V16, the P25 and that great V8. It would have been so much better to have closed it all down when BRM was at the top of the tree.

I reminded Sir Alfred of how Mercedes had ceased works participation in motor sport and some other companies too. In 1964, we had discussed this at length and I believe Sir Alfred

would have agreed to close down, but there were other pressures to be considered. Before the closure, I spent some time at Bourne and Folkingham, making sure that the last remaining P25 was, at least, a runner for the sale.

Knowing that there was one V16 Mark II BRM in reasonable condition and fearing that it might go abroad, I considered who might buy it over here. Tom Wheatcroft was a likely possibility and he had become a good friend of mine. We had even discussed the possibility of joining forces at the Donington Museum when it was being built, and I had given him a lot of help with the British Racing Partnership BRM, so I contacted Tom suggesting that he should buy the V16 – for England! Tom laughed but he said that he would think about it. I was abroad at the time of the sale but I was delighted to hear that Tom had bought it and even more delighted a little later when he let me drive it again.

I had known Elizabeth Junek, surely one of the greatest women racing drivers in the world, for many years. We corresponded regularly, but the international political situation after the Second World War prevented her from travelling to the West from her native Czechoslovakia. In 1969, that situation eased a little and, with help from Lord Montagu, a visa was procured enabling Elizabeth to come over for a holiday in England. I met her off the plane and she came to stay with us at Kineton for a week or so; then to the Rowleys in Staffordshire; and finally to Lord and Lady Montagu at Beaulieu. As a guest of the Bugatti Owners' Club and the Vintage Sports Car Club,

Above:
Mike Edmondson and Tony Hirst with their supercharged MG C-type at the Stratford-upon-Avon Motor Museum.

Above far right:
Rodney Walkerley with Elizabeth Junek and Penny.

she attended all their racing events during her stay. Despite her age, she drove my old Type 35 Bugatti and several other potent Bugattis, at great speed at Prescott and Oulton Park: a fabulous character, we all loved dearly. Remember Elizabeth was competing in first-class racing against the top drivers in the early 1920s!

Rivers storming up Shelsley Walsh in the BRM V16.

CHAPTER TWENTY FOUR

Interest in the vintage scene was escalating. I formed a small company restoring sports and racing cars at Bidford-on-Avon and my eldest son, Peter joined me after serving his apprenticeship at Rolls Royce at Derby. Peter and Mike Raahague ran the company as joint managing directors. I was the sleeping chairman because I am absolutely clueless on commercial matters.

Among several interesting projects we did the GKN four-wheel-drive Special with the 7-litre Chrysler "hemi" engine; the famous Jock Horsfall Spa 2-litre Aston Martin and a Le Mans type 4½-litre Bentley. The company, named Rivers-Fletcher – Raahague, provided me with the opportunity to construct the pre-war Alvis Speed 25 which I had planned for the 1939 Tourist Trophy race.

I found a running chassis and Peter took charge of the re-build and construction of the body to the design I laid down before the War.

Right from the first I loved that TT type Alvis and raced it in all the sprints and hillclimbs with a reasonable amount of success. The best achievement was FTD at an Alvis speed hillclimb on the test hill at Brooklands. In fact, this was the only speed event held at Brooklands since the War and only happened because of a loophole in Regulations since plugged.

Above left:
The four-wheel-drive GKN FF 100, an exciting project in 1973, when the author's son Peter and Mike Raahauge joined him at Bidford.

Above:
Final decisions on the bodylines of the Alvis Speed

Top:

Favourites old and new: Alvis Speed 25 and XJS at home.

Above:

The Kineton stable in 1980: Alvis Speed 25, Alvis 12/70 saloon, baby Railton, Ford Capri, and Hillman Imp.

Above right:

On top of the banking at Brooklands in the Alvis Speed 25.

The Brooklands Society used to organize a reunion at the Brooklands track every year. There was no racing, of course, but on the test hill and on a short stretch of banking, cleared by enthusiasts in the Society, there were demonstration runs in cars that were the same as or similar to those that raced before the Second World War at Brooklands. I enjoyed driving again some of the cars I had driven on the track in the 30s.

Both of my sons, Peter and Jeremy, competed in autocross. Jeremy had a variety of cars, including a Bantam and a very nice Dellow. Peter and his wife, Margaret, went the usual rounds of small sports cars and both competed with a Healey Sprite, which they still own. Then Peter got serious about it and bought a fine

Left:
With Meredith Owens in the Alvis Speed 25.

Opposite left:
Margaret Rivers Fletcher at Curborough in the frog-eyed Sprite.

Opposite right:
Peter in the 1100 Cooper-JAP with Margaret, their sons, William and Henry and a bearded friend.

Cooper 500 ex-C A N May with a JAP engine, which was followed by my old Cooper-JAP Mark 8 1100. He had eight years of successful sprints and hillclimbing with his Coopers. At that time I was driving my Speed 25 Alvis and a variety of racing cars for other people. Peter, Margaret and two grandsons used to join Penny and me for the racing at Prescott and Curborough. It was all very much a family affair with a third generation getting interested as well.

Working from home I greatly missed all the company facilities of telephone, teleprinter and secretarial services. I could not afford a full-time private secretary, but I was very lucky because Penny, through her activities in the local amateur dramatic society, met Stella Tompkins, who became my part-time secretary for many years. Energetic and enthusiastic, Stella persuaded me to write autobiographical motor racing books, an activity that became a very large slice of my life and income. Stella continues to look after my accounts, she and her family often joining us and helping at Prescott, typical of the extent to which I have always needed help – chaps to rebuild and prepare racing cars,

Left:
One he should have kept: Jeremy in his Dellow.

Above:
Stella Tompkins in the TT Lea-Francis Hyper Sport for the Stratford-upon-Avon Motor Museum.

secretaries to handle articles, books, films, travel and meetings, etc.

The film shows that I used to give on the old *Queen Mary* in the 1950s now led to much bigger ones on the new *Queen Elizabeth*. The arrangement was two shows per passage to and from New York, which gave me first-class accommodation as a guest of Cunard. At the instigation originally of John Dugdale, I made more visits to the United States in the 1970s – once or twice each year, each time spending a month or two over there.

In New York, there were parties and shows with René Dreyfus and other Bugatti and Bentley people. With Karen Miller and Jaguar Cars Inc., I did shows all over the Eastern States from Boston, Mass., to Washington, DC, and had drives at Lime Rock. Karen introduced me to Sherman Wolf, for whom I drove the Ferrari 625 that I had previously driven for Anthony Bamford at Prescott. In Detroit I met David Mouatt who became joint-owner with me of my Alvis Speed Twenty-Five. He drove this car very well at a sprint at a Brooklands reunion before I shipped it across to America on the *Queen Elizabeth II*. It now lives in Detroit, so that David and I can drive it in events in Michigan.

In Smithtown, New York: Richard Bowman in his one-off 1½-litre SS Jaguar, originally built for the late John Lyons.

Below left:
David Mouatt with the Alvis Speed 25 on a trailer for Detroit; in the background the *Queen Elizabeth II.*

Below:
With Victor Louis in his 4¼-litre Bentley at his dacha near Moscow.

All my activities in California are arranged by my friend Mark Mayuga, who is the president of the Jaguar Club in Long Beach. A dynamic organizer, Mark has arranged shows and promotions for me all over the Western seaboard from San Diego to San Francisco, including a C-type Jaguar drive at Laguna Seca. We also did a 2000-mile trip from Los Angeles through Oklahoma to the Ozarks and Chicago, one of the longest and most enjoyable

Above:
In a typical left-hand-drive Mallelieu Bentley.

Right:
Rebuilding Crewe Bentleys at Mallelieu Engineering, Abingdon.

drives. I shared the wheel with Mark Mayuga, who is a fine co-driver.

Penny and I were going to have a holiday in Russia, staying with friends at the British Embassy in Moscow. I got off on the wrong foot, for I had forgotten my passport. I then tried to get through passport control at Moscow airport with a photostat copy. Officials at London Airport had warned me that, although I was a VIP visitor to the Embassy, the Russian authorities would be unlikely to let me in. Penny passed through safely with her passport, but I was manhandled and officially deported via the British plane which was held back for my ignominious return.

After a lot more drama I was eventually able to return and join Penny at the British Embassy. To my surprise, I met a charming English-speaking Russian diplomat, Victor Louis, who owned the only pre-war Bentley in Russia. He was a member of the Bentley Drivers' Club and I had a great time with him,

visiting him and his family at their lovely dacha and driving his 1938 $4\frac{1}{4}$-litre Bentley with an Erdmann and Rossi drophead coupé body. Some time later I arranged for this car to be properly restored in England and Victor and I have been friends ever since.

Three years' consultancy with Mallelieu at Abingdon gave me thousands of miles of Bentley motoring, because I road-tested all the firm's Bentleys. They were interesting cars, very well engineered but undergeared. Too many were tarted up with pseudo racing equipment, but some were delightful tourers in very good taste. After the company failed, the good workforce carried on for some time restoring historic and classic MGs.

Above:
Don Young in the Delage greeting the author at a gas station on the freeway at Santa Barbara, Calif.

Above right:
Before our race around Santa Barbara.

Right:
Karen Miller with her XK120 at Watkins Glen, the car the author should have driven!

Bryan Corse's fastest cars – C, D, XKSS, lightweight E-type and the XJS.

However, as many of us have found out, restoration is so labour-intensive that it is very difficult to make it pay.

For two or three years most of my motoring and racing was all MG with an ex-works MGA coupé and an MG BGT: there were many Prescott hillclimbs and, in America, the New England "T" Register events.

I sold the MGA to Val Christianson who is a rabid enthusiast with several other MGs. He has become a good friend, sharing the same enthusiasms and is a very good and sensitive driver. He keeps the MGA in our blue livery and joins us for some of the events where I sometimes take the wheel again.

I made some more visits to the United States, travelling each way on the *Queen Elizabeth 2* presenting talks and film shows featuring Jaguar cars. All these promotions were arranged with Jaguar Cars, Coventry and Jaguar Cars Inc, New York.

Later I did further shows for the Bentley Drivers' Club at the Briggs Cunningham Automotive Museum in San Diego through Dr C I Conrad and others through Bob Turner in Chicago.

At Santa Barbara I stayed with Don Young. He met me at a gas station on the freeway, driving his ex-Malcolm Campbell 1½-litre Delage. We had an unofficial two-lap race on the freeways and byroads of Santa Barbara. Don drove his Type 35 Grand Prix Bugatti and I the Delage. We were not hanging about, but were nevertheless cheered on by the police as they held back the other private cars and coaches. To us in Britain this all sounds impossible, but it did really happen.

There were more meetings and shows with Phil Hill and a chance to race Karen Miller's XK 120 at Watkins Glen. To my shame I have to admit that I only practised, finding that I just could not cope in the fast company of Don Redman and others on the Watkins Glen circuit. I had forgotten that it had been 30 years since I had raced on a circuit among other cars, having concentrated on sprints and hillclimbs for all that time. However, I was able to watch Karen, one of the best women drivers, certainly one of the most attractive, get a fine third place in a fast race behind a D-type and a C-type Jaguar.

Since I have written a book on the Jaguar XJS and driven a lot of fast cars, Jaguar Limited and Jaguar Cars Inc. usually provide me with a car for all my foreign travel, as well as for quite a lot of promotions over here.

After the untimely death of Sir Alfred Owen his sons David and John carried on the business of the Group and we kept in

Below left:
One of the author's favourite Jaguars, the XJS Eventer.

Below:
With Bob Tullius and the Group 44 Jaguar at Winchester, Va.

Above:
The author drives Sally Marsh's ERA R1B, the famous ex-Dick Seaman/Billy Cotton car at Brooklands, demonstrating the line taken by Raymond Mays when he broke the Mountain Circuit record.

Above right:
The ex-Earl Howe ERA R8C, beautifully restored and splendidly driven by Bruce Spollon.

Right:
Neil Corner.

Far right:
Nick Mason.

Some of the fast men: Colin and Anthony Mayman, Bruce Spollon and Rodney Felton at Oulton Park.

touch with developments. As vintage and historic events increased in scope and so many of the Bourne cars were restored and raced with ever-increasing success, Sir Alfred's family took a new interest in BRM appearing in vintage and historic events.

David Owen came to Shelsley Walsh to see me drive Tom Wheatcroft's Mark II V16 BRM on the occasion of the unveiling of the Raymond Mays memorial. Having been employed by the Owen organization and BRM for the most important part of my life, it gives me the greatest pleasure to be retained by the Owen group as a consultant today. David Owen, the Chairman, has so many of his father's qualities, including an absolute honesty, (unusual these days), and a keen sense of humour. These qualities and others make for a happy ship – for me that is what it is all about.

Guy Spollon, the son of Bruce Spollon who owns and races the ex-Earl Howe ERA R8C, took over the secretaryship of the ERA Club. The 1980s saw ERAs and the ERA Club buoyant in every respect. ERAs dominate in all the vintage and historic events; while the club retains its own selectivity, its membership consisting only of those who have a special enthusiasm for these great pre-war road-racing cars.

In today's professional racing, people keep on complaining, there are no great characters, no one like Freddie Dixon, Charles Brackenbury, Duncan Hamilton, Innes Ireland or Mike Hawthorn and no great historians like Rodney Walkerley. That is probably true - in the professional sector. Of course, people are going to the wrong races. They should be at the vintage and historic motor events. We have all the great characters now, as varied as ever and every bit as fast and hairy. There was the late Patrick Lindsay and now his son, Ludovic, Neil Corner, Bruce Spollon, Martin Morris, Willie Green, Nick Mason, Rodney Felton, Bill Morris and others, as well as the one who seems unbeatable today: Anthony Mayman. As for the writers no one could be more outspoken than Denis Jenkinson, Eoin Young and Doug Nye.

We revere the earlier Grand Prix heroes, Nuvolari, Caracciola, Rosemeyer, Farina, Seaman, Mays, Moss, Hawthorn, Collins, Fangio, Gonzalez; and a little later, both of the Hills (Phil and Graham), Jim Clark, Jack Brabham, Jackie Stewart and company. I know their races were full Grand Prix events, whereas those of today are much shorter and are not important nationally let alone internationally. Yet I am taking away nothing from our old heroes when I honestly consider that Mayman and the other drivers of his calibre today are every bit as great as the old ones – and of course better because every decade, performances in all the sports are improved. Look at the record books; competitors run, ride, drive and swim faster, and jump higher. In fact, most of us drive better than our fathers or mothers.

Every decade has to show the improvements needed to match modern technology. Technology does not wait around in the laboratory or on the proving ground. It races ahead so fast that we old buffers do not even see it go. So although you may be a better driver than your parents, do not get too pleased about it; your children will make rings round you.

It is well said that comparisons are odious; they can be worse than odious if you try to compare drivers of different eras.

Vintage races today are so like similar events at Brooklands, Donington and Crystal Palace before the war. Just the same ERAs, Maseratis, Altas and MGs. Just as I was close to Raymond Mays and his mechanic Ken Richardson with the ERA R4D, so I am as close to Anthony Mayman and Jim Fitzgerald with R4D today. History repeats itself.

As the cars are warmed up at Silverstone, scraps of conversation with Jim Fitzgerald are just like those with Ken Richardson before the war at Brooklands. On the grid, Anthony is fairly tense, determined to lead the pack into Copse; Ray used to be just as tense and determined to head the field into Dunlop's Delight. There is the same similarity about the rest of the grid: Bruce, on R8C, noncommital, as was Lord Howe; Ludovic just as professional as "B. Bira" was; and all of them conscious of the threat of the relatively new man, Duncan Ricketts – as the drivers had all felt 50 years ago about young Tony Rolt.

On the grid at Silverstone with Bruce Halford, Anthony Mayman in R4D and Jim Fitzgerald.

Today, happy as a sandboy running over to congratulate Anthony Mayman on each victory, I feel just as I did in the same situation with Raymond Mays in 1939. For further emphasis I could extend the story back to 1931, with Ray and his Invicta on the Mountain circuit at Brooklands. In a sense, nothing changes.

CHAPTER TWENTY FIVE

Through Bugattis at Prescott I met Jennifer Waters a relative of my friend Jack Warner (PC Dixon of Dock Green) and his sister Elsie and Doris Waters.

Once again the same stage/motor racing connection. Jennifer came to many racing events and helped with many film shows. I developed a close friendship with Richard McCann whose experience with Bentleys, the Caesar Special, Lagonda and MG matched my enthusiasm.

Left:
Uwe Hucke and Jennifer Walters with the four-wheel-drive Bugatti at Shelsley Walsh.

Right:
A very fast Alvis man, Albert Sparrowhawk, in his 4.3 alongside the author's Speed 25 at Prescott.

With the Alvis Speed 25 permanently in America I replaced it with another very similar Alvis – a 1934 Speed 20. By that time, our company, Rivers-Fletcher – Raahague had finished with the restoration of cars and Peter and Mike were busy building sidecars and trailers for motor cycles; not quite so much fun but more lucrative. So my Speed 20 was constructed by Automobile Restorations. Like many such projects it took longer than I planned to get it right, but it is now very much to my liking. It was restored and fitted with a light two-seater racing body almost to the same design as my TT Speed 25, the body being built near Bourne by a craftsman who had been at BRM.

Richard and I shared a lot of the driving including a most enjoyable week in the Isle of Man with the VSCC. He so liked the Alvis that I designed for him a similar body for his 1934 3½-litre Bentley which was in the throes of a ground-up restoration. It was at that time that we first thought of a team, our cars in the same livery, like the private teams I so enjoyed pre-war.

Over the last 20 years I had seen the occasional Grand Prix,

but no longer being involved in a team I felt rather out of it. Each year I knew fewer people in the pit lane. I did not like the direction Grand Prix was taking, sponsorship having a very big say. I kept on saying that I would ignore it, as my friend George Monkhouse does, but dammit! I cannot quite do that. The skill and bravery of the drivers, the fantastic speeds, the high level of technology – all demand such admiration; but I cannot accept the bad behaviour, the lack of sportsmanship, the show-biz razzamatazz and the financial budget to support it. I.feel that I must be a cad regretting the popularity and undoubted success of today's racing. I feel that I should be glad that the sport is now available to a much larger public – but I do not like it at all. It must be my age; I resent that popularity. Somehow it devalues the currency. Too many people in the Paddock and mostly the wrong people.

It seems only a short time ago when George Monkhouse and I used to walk all round the Monaco circuit during the Grand Prix, filming from the track itself and even crossing it when we wanted!

I know it would be impossible today, but I also know that as we lost our freedom with necessary restrictions I liked it less and regretted even more the passing of the gentleman's sport of the 20s and 30s.

Having lived and loved Grand Prix motor racing, seen it disappear, then helped to resurrect it. I lived and loved it more than ever, I rejoiced in its success at the top of the tree but now find that I am out of my depth – it is no longer my scene.

I have no tears for Grand Prix racing, but only admiration for Denis Jenkinson who still loves it. My excuse that he is ten years my junior is not really valid, as I know he will never change. So leaving, but not quite forgetting the Grands Prix, let us consider sports car racing.

Once upon a time, you could buy a sports car from the showroom, use it on the road and, if you were good enough, race it in principal events like Le Mans and the Tourist Trophy – once upon a time! When I was in the sales department of Bentley Motors in 1930, private owners could order Bentleys to Le Mans specification. We called them semi-Le Mans, or Le Mans replicas.

Of course, they were not absolutely to the current Le Mans specification; it was realised and accepted that the works cars were always a bit faster. There was the further excuse that works cars would be, to some extent, experimental so could not be safely sold to the public.

There was no fixed price for a Le Mans replica model. Indeed it was not catalogued as such. Each customer specified which items would be required – big fuel tank, quick-action filler caps, hour-glass pistons, stoneguards, high-ratio back axles, straight-tooth axles, racing brake adjusters, large diameter instruments and so on. No two Le Mans replicas were exactly the same. Incidentally, I cannot remember anyone in those days wanting a standard Bentley but looking like a Le Mans model. I am afraid that the dreadful 'look-alike' disease is a relatively modern illness.

At Bentley, our replica cars were suitable for top-class racing. For example, both Sir Henry Birkin and Humphrey Cook bought such cars and ran them in the Tourist Trophy race in 1930. This was, of course, before the supercharged 4½-litre cars sponsored by the Hon. Dorothy Paget.

Some years later, when I was with another company, I demonstrated and sold Alvis, Riley and MG sports cars which private owners ran on the road as well as racing them in sports car events. I remember that some time in 1935 or 1936 we had a secondhand C-Type MG. It was supercharged and had all the right racing equipment, but was a perfectly standard production model that was catalogued. The first owner had purchased it straight out of the showroom of University Motors in London.

At Brooklands with Richard McCann watching the old bikes going off for their demonstration runs.

In due course I was able to interest one of my friends in the car and a trial run was arranged. Since the car was required for competition, the obvious venue for a trial run was Brooklands track. As I was a member of the Brooklands Automobile Racing Club I decided that we would take the car down to the track for the demonstration. There were no problems driving to Weybridge using a light throttle, not too many revs and running on 'soft' warming-up plugs.

In the Paddock at Brooklands we put in a set of harder plugs for high speed. Having ascertained that only a couple of bikes were using the track, I knew that they would not be in our way, nor we in theirs, as bikes seldom used the banking. My customer was not a member of the Club so I drove him for three or four laps on the outer circuit.

I took the car slowly up the hill to the Home Banking, turned left on to the Outer Circuit and we pulled into the first bay before the Railway Straight. After waiting to see the bikes go by, we set off towards the Byfleet Banking. Using a maximum of 5500 rpm, I pushed the gear lever into top at about 60 mph.

We did our lapping at about 85 mph, which may sound very slow by modern standards, but in those days in a little 750 cc racing sports car it was quite exciting. My customer was very pleased with the performance and we returned to London to complete the sale. What a lovely way to earn one's living! How we miss Brooklands today! However, the track is now in good hands and, with the Brooklands Trust under the chairmanship of Sir Peter Masefield, the restoration of part of the track and the clubhouse is assured for a live museum and a place of demonstration for the motor car, motorcycle and aviation world.

The examples of the situation at Bentley and cars like the C-Type MG were typical of the situation pre-war. Sports car racing, whether it was international top-class events such as the Tourist Trophy and Le Mans, or club events at Donington, was for cars which could be used on the road and the cars were driven on the road to the events.

Left:
At Brooklands with the Alvis Speed 25.

Right:
With Sir Peter Masefield and the Alvis Speed 20 at Brooklands.

Now surely the same situation should exist today? Racing a car in a Grand Prix, or any other formula, is another thing altogether. Sports car racing, however, should be for cars which we recognise and to which we can relate. Let us consider the Le Mans 24-hour race, probably the world's greatest sports car race. First of all, what would we lose if the regulations demanded absolutely legal road-going vehicles with MOT and other requirements? We would lose just a little speed. Only a little because, within a year or two, modern technology would make up the loss. Anyway, speed is relative and the loss of spectacle would be marginal. In any case the speed is now extremely dangerous and it would be a good thing if it could be reduced.

There would, of course, be the problem of enforcing rules to prevent racing cars masquerading as sports cars. Homologation would have to be strictly enforced and the number of cars produced would have to be much larger to make it impractical for any manufacturer to produce cars for racing only. I do not deny that today's racing sports cars are splendid vehicles, often producing fine racing, but I claim that they are misnomers. I believe that the production and development of these cars has been along the wrong lines. If the over-riding and first requirement of the regulations had always been that the cars must be 'street-legal', to be taxed, insured and driven to the events, then we would have had sports racing cars developed on the right lines.

Once upon a time a code of honour helped to keep motor racing a sport rather than big business. I know that one cannot put the clock back, but I am sure that today's nearly free-for-all regulations for sports cars tends to produce the wrong sort of car. I believe that, in the long run, the racing of 'street cars' would benefit everyone, manufactuers and customers alike.

The other day I drove a TWR-modified Jaguar XJS from its home base at Kidlington, near Oxford, to Silverstone and to Donington. I drove that car quite slowly in heavy traffic on the road and as fast as I could on the circuits. This was the model with the Getrag five-speed manual gearbox, up-rated engine and much tighter suspension. It was, of course, absolutely legal and in fact, nearly as flexible and quiet as the standard production car.

For racing, the car would have to be lightened and no doubt would have no trim. A roll cage would have to be fitted. The most important item would be the tyres. Of course, no slicks would be allowed and since all the tyres would have to conform to the MOT regulations, there would presumably not be so much difference between tyres for wet weather and dry weather. Again, the amount of noise would have to be reduced to conform with Road Traffic Act requirements. None of these items should present any real difficulty.

David Black and his wife change a wheel on this marvellous Alfa Romeo monoposto at Silverstone before the author's drive in it. This model was too fast for the author – he is more confident with the Monza – but a great experience.

In the old days, I remember that everything was not always perfect. Some racing cars masquerading as sports cars got into the principal events. Even Monoposto Alfa Romeos with wings and lights ran in the Mille Miglia against real sports Monza Alfas. But at least a real attempt was made to keep sports cars genuinely road-going. When did we lose our way? Probably in the late 1950s when sports cars started to arrive at events on trailers or in transporters.

I am afraid we lost our way in many other sports in another direction and that was nothing to do with regulations. The whole meaning of sport has changed direction. Perhaps this was inevitable with sponsorship which went hand-in-hand with increased popularity and television coverage. In my opinion the dictum that in sporting contests what matters most is not whether you win or lose but how you play the game is right. On television a little while ago, Bunny Austin, one-time tennis ace, spoke very eloquently on the deplorable lack of sportsmanship in nearly every direction today. In his day, the umpire's decision was never queried and in all sports defeat was taken with good grace and success modestly accepted. I used to watch and love first-class cricket at Lords. Players like Patsy Hendren scoring a century would modestly acknowledge applause from the crowd and a quiet "well done" from the other batsman by merely touching his cap. Similar attitudes applied in other sports. Today, however, defeat is seldom gracefully accepted. Umpires and referees' decisions are queried, while even the mildest success is greeted with cheers, hugs and kisses which seem to me to be in the worst possible taste.

This last bleat of mine about sportsmanship and bad taste may be something that we cannot do anything about. Perhaps it doesn't matter, perhaps the standards that appeal to me are just old-hat and do not apply today.

With Hans Herrmann in the 1955 Mille Miglia Mercedes at Donington: this was about the fastest drive the author enjoyed as a passenger. Behind the car are "Jumbo" Goddard and Eoin Young.

But surely my point about sports cars is viable today: I repeat – sports car racing should be for real road-going sports cars.

How lucky I was that just about the time that I quit Grand Prix and other forms of modern motor racing, the vintage and classic scene started to bloom. We owe so much to the VSCC, where everything is competitive but fun – not an easy combination to achieve but so worthwhile. The vintage scene is so good that I hesitate to criticize, but one should beware of avarice. We do not buy a vintage car for investment, (unless we are in the trade), any more that we would walk on the wrong side of a lady on the sidewalk. Greed and a lowering of standards have the potential to spoil the vintage scene.

Originality has become something of a fetish, tending to spoil the fun. I was on the committee of the VSCC in the old days when Forrest Lycett was the president and Laurence Pomeroy was the president elect. We had a relaxed and tolerant attitude towards originality which worked very well. Many famous old cars were happily accepted and raced as vintage to everyone's pleasure. For example –

1927 Delage Grand Prix 1½-litre (Benoist, Campbell, Howe,

Seaman) rebuilt by Chula in 1938 (Bira); new chassis with IFS, etc;

1931 Bentley 8-litre Forrest Lycett. Over many years completely rebuilt and modernised 1937-47;

1925 Sunbeam 4-litre V12 racing car (Seagrave 1926 world records) 1928 Kaye Don at Brooklands (painted red and named 'Tiger'). Very successful Outer Circuit Brooklands history. 1932 re-built for Sir Malcolm Campbell. New chassis, pre-selector gearbox, hydraulic brakes, etc. Raced by Campbell with success at Brooklands and elsewhere (painted blue and called Sunbeam 1).

The Delage was raced after the war by John Rowley, a president of the VSCC. In 1950 he won the GP Itala Trophy for vintage racing cars. The car has been raced by others in recent vintage events and is universally revered as a famous vintage racing car.

The Lycett Bentley has been continuously developed and modernised throughout the period 1937-47, using modern postwar materials and many modern components, but retaining its splendid vintage character. It is now in the appreciative hands of Jack Sears and regarded as one of the greatest vintage Bentleys.

The 4-litre V12 Sunbeam was rebuilt several times after the war and raced by many. Latterly it was rebuilt basically to Malcolm Campbell's specification, called 'Tiger', (I consider wrongly), and painted red, (if we were fussy about originality it should be blue or green).

If we consider our sport to be just for enjoyment and are not concerned with investment, then we can happily accept the Delage, the Bentley and the Sunbeam together with many other cars with vintage origins as Vintage – why not? Nevertheless, if we have this happy relaxed tolerant attitude, then of course we must apply it to other cars.

If you prefer cars as original as possible, that is fine and much admired. However, if others do not share exactly the same view, be tolerant. In racing you just have to be tolerant – I have listed just three cars but I could go on and on, listing most of the field. If we were fussy I could make nonsense of the well documented racing history of the VSCC.

So, as we accepted and loved great cars with vintage and historic origins and continue to do so in the the future – then we must be tolerant of lesser items not quite correct for cars' dates of manufacture.

As ever, some cars are faster because of modern improvements, (even more are faster because the drivers are quicker!), but so what! We certainly do not want all the cars exactly the same like modern formulate.

It is impossible to tie up rules for eligibility completely. How we played the game over the years seems best – a general date of the car and a trust in the honesty and sportsmanship of the owner. I have known and know today just about as many of our vintage drivers as anyone and I consider the sportsmanship and integrity of our vintage drivers to be as high as ever.

As in every activity there have always been a few rogues and cheats, but they have not achieved much. So let us not spoil it all by getting too fussy about little things. If we delve too deeply, we will find that no car is really acceptable!

President of the Vintage Sports Car Club: Roger Collings in his Mercedes with the other fine Edwardians.

There is another aspect of originality which may be a problem – the replica. The word is used to mean so many different things. Personally I have nothing against a really good replica which must be nearly as good as the original. That certainly applies to the replica 'C' type Jaguar which I drove at Laguna Seca. Anything less than a real replica can pose a problem but the splendid specials produced by Lynx and some others are fine cars well engineered.

I have been driving Anthony Mayman's replica ERA "AJM 1" splendidly built by Tony Merrick who is a superb restorer. I love this car and in fact, it is a good deal more original than any of the other "genuine" ERAs on the circuit today!

On the vintage scene there is plenty of room for different viewpoints. Some of my friends demand almost complete originality; I go for much less. None of us is right or wrong.

Perhaps I have an advantage over you because I am so old. I loved them then and drove them when they were brand new so that is the way I like to see them today.

Perhaps you should think carefully why you love the old cars? Surely it should be how they look, feel and go. Do you really mind about the chassis number if everything else is right? I must admit that there is something about a car whose history is special to you, cars I have raced and loved. Perhaps chassis numbers are important, anyhow more important now than I used to think.

I am still a disciple of SCH Davis, who taught us what motor sport was all about many years ago. In his last letter to me, just before his death, he wrote urging me to carry on his work. Since I am only just another enthusiast, I probably do not carry all that much weight, but I am sure that the work of the Vintage Sports Car Club promotes the sporting spirit of Sammy Davis.

There has to be some advantage to being around for a long time. One rather nice thing for me is the fact that I can remember a lot of the views expressed by some of the 'greats' – Sammy Davis, George Eyston, Campbell, Howe, Mays, etc. They taught me to love our cars, not to thrash them and certainly not to damage them. They taught us to drive as sportsmen, caring how we play the game more than winning.

Our sport is pretty good these days – let us try to keep it that way. We surely do not want too many new boys in the game; they would not understand our sport – they would be more interested in investments. I think we got it about right at Brooklands, with our "right crowd and no crowding".

The author drove both of these at the 1988 Classic Prescott: Anthony Mayman's ERA and his own Alvis.

Top:
The author driving Val Christensen's 'Replica' Jaguar 'D' type at Prescott 1991.

Above:
Rivers Fletcher Team Speed 20 Alvis cars, showing the author's sports-touring model and Shirley in her lightweight car, 1991.

CHAPTER TWENTY SIX

Although I was heavily involved with other matters, I did notice that rather a lot of good people had left the administration of the Brooklands Society. There seemed to be some dissension. When Lord Montagu alerted me that things were going wrong, I was called to a meeting with the representatives of Surrey County Council and the main companies owning or leasing parts of Brooklands. Indeed, things had come to a pretty pass by the time a Trust was appointed under the chairmanship of Sir Peter Masefield. This was the Peter Masefield I had met through Lord Brabazon 40 years ago, who helped us with the Monaco aero-engine and later arranged for us to use wartime airfields for motor racing.

Sir Peter had risen to the top of the aeronautical world and because of his position in that sphere he was appointed chairman of the Brooklands Trust. It was fortituous that he had also been very interested in motor racing, as well as a close friend of the late Whitney Straight.

With great skill and tact, Sir Peter achieved the near miracle of putting the Brooklands society in better order. He backed the development of a splendid museum in the old Brooklands clubhouse under an excellent manager, now the director, Morag Barton. Today Sir Peter masterminds the mammoth project of rebuilding a lot of the old track and aerodrome for a permanent live museum for the car, motorcycle and aircraft worlds. On his Brooklands Council I see this project is of great importance and will require all our efforts.

As I look back on the last half of my 60 year involvement in motor racing, I try to pick the cars that I have loved best. Without doubt, the BRM V16 was the most exciting. The Jaguar XJ13 was probably the fastest sports car, but I only just got the feel of it and did not drive it at any real speed. Nor did I really extend the Walkinshaw-modified Jaguar XJS, although I did have a bit of a go at Silverstone, and I think this should be the best modern sports/racing car for the road.

While we are with the moderns – postwar cars at least – I must consider my Cooper 1100s. I had most success with those

Getting into the Jaguar XJ13.

Above:
Mark V Cooper-JAP 1100.

Above far right:
Different noses at Coventry:
Alvis Speed 25, Jaguar XJ13
and XJS.

cars: great little projectiles. But I did not keep on going to have a look at them, as I did with my HWM Jaguar. That car I certainly loved. It almost killed me, but that fits, surely? One would die for true love – and I very nearly did.

I have driven quite a few good postwar machines. The BRM P25 is among the best, as is the Lotus Type 18. However, I was very conscious all the time of the fact that they were really too fast for me. I did not begin to do them justice. When I drove the V16 BRM at Shelsley Walsh I was not too worried, because everyone knew that the car was an enormous handful, so no one expected me to break any records. I gave it all I could as far as the Crossing, then I chickened out and toured up.

In fact, my favourite postwar racing car was a rival to the BRM P25: the Ferrari 625 that I drove at Prescott for Anthony Bamford and at Lime Rock for Sherman Wolf. The 625 felt just

Driving the P25 BRM.

right, beautifully balanced and entirely predictable. Bruce Halford, who has wide experience of both the Ferrari and BRM, tells me that if I had driven both cars to the limit, I would have discovered that the BRM was the better machine. I believe this, since Bruce is an excellent driver and very knowledgeable about all the cars, but I could not prove it because I am not good enough to find out.

Needless to say all my real favourites are pre-war cars. There were the famous Bentley Le Mans Sixes, and Barnato's Blue Train Speed Six coupé, which I was so pleased to see again in 1988 in Bob Cole's good hands in San Francisco. My other close favourite was the Bugatti 57SC Atlantic, which Barry Price let me have for a week in 1980. Then there was the unforgettable ex-Malcolm Campbell 38/250 Mercedes which I drove in 1945; more recently the present owner, Ronald Stern, generously entered me to drive it in an event. Earl Howe's favourite Brooklands car, the Bugatti Type 59 which Sir Ralph Millais let me drive at Prescott, was absolutely fantastic. I think this is the best-looking racing car in the world. Although I cannot really love so modern a car, I think the 1964 Formula 1 BRM Type 126 is just about as beautiful as that sort of car can be.

To me, the most beautiful sports car is still the 1930 Invicta 4½-litre low chassis with Carbodies open sports body. I covered my own involvement with this model in the book *Mostly Motor*

Above far left:
Ronald Stern in his ex-Malcolm Campbell Mercedes 38/250 at Silverstone.

Above far right:
The Hon. Amschel Rothschild in the P25 BRM at Silverstone.

Below far left:
Driving the Ferrari at Lime Rock.

Below far right:
In the author's opinion, the most beautiful pre-war racing car. Craig in the Bugatti Type 59 at Prescott, 1939.

Racing. Now Invicta has come back into my life with Donald Monro's daughter, Shirley, joining us at Prescott and finding "Red Gauntlet" being restored in Devon, and with another lady driver who is also having great success with that model – Jo Moss – who most generously let me drive her Invicta at Shelsley Walsh – after more than 50 years. Although now beyond my slender purse, the ERA has been, from its very inception, part of my life.

For me, driving an ERA on a circuit or on a hillclimb is the ultimate motor racing experience. Some cars are faster, some have better roadholding, but no other car thrills me as much. There is something special about an ERA: your position at the wheel, looking down on that long louvred bonnet with the wheels sticking out well on each side; the controlling of wheelspin: the handling on the corners holding the tail out; the firm ride and the noise; and of course the appearance. Younger drivers used to sitting further down in the car, with modern suspension, feel that you are too exposed in an ERA, but I like it that way. The great example is Raymond May's famous R4D, now owned and driven by Anthony Mayman, aged 39 – the same age as Ray when he was at the zenith of his racing career, just before the Second World War. Anthony is now winning everything and breaking all the records, just as Raymond Mays did. R4D is a great credit to Jim Fitzgerald and Geoff Squirrel, who prepare it so well. Anthony's generosity in letting me drive it at Silverstone and Prescott is beyond any words of mine. He is the kindest and most modest person, lending his cars to his friends and going out of his way to help other drivers.

Antony Mayman in his ERA R4D in a perfect full-throttle drift at Cadwell Park, 1990.

I had never been very interested in Veteran or even Edwardian cars, but when I was in San Diego CI Conrad took me to see a beautiful bright-yellow Mercer Raceabout of 1913 in a private collection, I fell for it straight away. To my delight and surprise,

VSCC Weston Speed Trial 1990. Jo Moss in the Invicta (25) and Shirley Monro-Dickson in the Alvis (34).

Brian Lewis, the young owner of the collection, got it out for me and fired it up so that I could have a drive. It was really superb: easy and straightforward to drive and very like any European vintage sports car of the 1920s. The high-geared steering was remarkably light and there was immense torque from walking pace from its 300-inch 4-cylinder engine with its unusual T-head side valves. It had a lovely gearbox with rather widely spaced ratios, only requiring normal double-declutching. Only the brakes required knowing. The footbrake did nothing except make a hissing noise; it was the handbrake that was normally used on the road.

As I have already indicated, I was most impressed by the friendly Californian police, who cheered and waved me on to the fast lane of the freeway. All this in an unlicensed, uninsured and quite illegal Mercer racing car! As the senior police officer said to me when he examined the car afterwards, "The law is laid down for ordinary road cars, but this is quite different". What an enlightened and sensible attitude!

As so many of my old motor racing friends are no longer with us, I am reminded that in this, my eightieth year I am lucky to be so fit so far, able to live a very active life, travel the world and still drive racing cars. Lucky too being married to my wife Penny, who has always supported my racing now our Golden Wedding Anniversary. However, with ever- increasing activity I have let some opportunities go by and the potential of some situations have not been realized. I have been missing things.

What to do? How to cope? Most of my family say, "Cut it down; time you reduced the activity". Absolutely justified and good sensible advice. But dammit! I am not that sensible and I cannot reduce. My mind goes the other way, looking forward to increasing. I know that I have always been dependent on good friends and now I find that I need even more help.

I think we have the answer. What used to be a "one man band" has developed into the Rivers Fletcher Motor Racing Team. About half a dozen friends sharing the load and the fun – that is the plan. The team will comprise my Alvis, Richard McCann's Bentley and Lagonda, Shirley Monro-Dickson, not with an Invicta but in her Alvis Speed 20, Val Christianson and his MGA, replica 'D' type and 'C' type Jaguars Keith Barnet with fine Aston Martin and Alvis experience and Jennifer Waters, (when we are able to drag her away from Bugattis).

These younger members of the team will usually do the driving of the faster cars, but all of us will be involved driving or supporting one another at events. All the Alvis, Bentley, Jaguar and MG will be in the same blue livery, as were some of our private équipes before the war. As the patron, I am happy to drive the slower cars, remembering how in our ERA team, our patron Humphrey Cook was happy to drive the 1100 while Raymond Mays and Pat Fairfield drove the faster 1½-litre cars.

It is my philosophy that when you are enjoying a good innings and make a century, you do not give up – you go on for another hundred. You may look back on a lot of good times – but no! that is wrong. You do not look back, you should just glance back. You look forward, forward to even better things ahead.

Above and right:
The Mercer Raceabout.

The situation looks brighter all the time. Vintage and historic racing is buoyant all over the world. Rivers Fletcher Motor Racing is beginning to take off. For me the 1990s are full of promise although it is a bit late in the day. Perhaps I am a late developer, or is it just the standard excuse for someone who never makes it. There will be more books, articles, television videos and promotions. I will be back on the QE2! Even more important, however, there will be more driving racing cars.

It is the future that is important, so let us fold down the main windscreen, put up a little aeroscreen and put the right foot hard down on the loud pedal. Easy now – not too much wheelspin and we are off in the 1990s. A well-known racing driver has just reminded me that 50 years ago I ended a lecture and an article in the *Autocar* with the words, "The noise, the smell and the people". Thank heaven nothing really changes – as ever it is "the noise, the smell and the people".

INDEX